basic PROJECTS

Game Maker

> David Waller

www.payne-gallway.co.uk

✓ Free online support
✓ Useful weblinks
✓ 24 hour online ordering

01865 888070

PAYNE-GALLWAY
Part of Pearson

Payne-Gallway is an imprint of Pearson Education Limited, a company incorporated in England and Wales, having its registered office at Edinburgh Gate, Harlow, Essex, CM20 2JE. Registered company number: 872828

www.payne-gallway.co.uk

Text © David Waller 2009

First published 2009

13 12 11 10 09
10 9 8 7 6 5 4 3 2 1

British Library Cataloguing in Publication Data
A catalogue record for this book is available from the British Library.

ISBN 978 1 905292 57 8

Designed by Wooden Ark Studios
Edited and typeset by Sparks – www.sparkspublishing.com
Cover design by Wooden Ark Studios
Printed in the UK by Scotprint

Acknowledgements
Every effort has been made to contact copyright holders of material reproduced in this book. Any omissions will be rectified in subsequent printings if notice is given to the publishers.

Websites
The websites used in this book were correct and up-to-date at the time of publication. It is essential for tutors to preview each website before using it in class so as to ensure that the URL is still accurate, relevant and appropriate. We suggest that tutors bookmark useful websites and consider enabling students to access them through the school/college intranet.

Ordering Information
Payne-Gallway, FREEPOST (OF1771),
PO Box 381, Oxford OX2 8BR
Tel: 01865 888070
Fax: 01865 314029
Email: orders@payne-gallway.co.uk

CONTENTS

So you know ...

This book is all about making computer games. Creating a computer game is far more fun than just playing one! You can use your imagination to design the characters and rooms where the game is set, plus you get to make up all of the rules. You can set what will happen when an object collides with another one – will it explode, gain more energy or change its appearance?

You can decide how many lives a character has and how many points are needed to move up to the next level. It's completely up to you!

We will be using software called **Game Maker**. This software is available at the website **http://www.yoyogames.com** and is free to download and use. Details of how to download and install the software are given in the next section. The software uses a graphical interface to allow us to program all of the actions, so we don't have to learn a new programming language. We just have to understand and plan what we want to happen. Using Game Maker to design and create games will allow you to show your capability in all of the strands of the National Curriculum.

The skills you will learn are:

> Task 1: How to create a new game, add objects and sprites, program events and actions, and keep the score.

> Task 2: How to add a splash screen, multiple levels and restart the game.

> Task 3: How to change an object's sprite during a game, set and keep track of the number of lives, and move to the next level.

> Task 4: How to replace one object with another during a game, use animated sprites and use variables. (Sprites are the graphic images used on screen to represent the objects used in the game. For example, each 'alien' object is represented by an image of a burger in Figure Intro.1. Variables are labels used to represent numbers. For example, you could have a variable called 'score' that would start at zero and then increase by one every time you hit an alien.)

You are eventually going to create a game to meet a design specification that you will be given. This will allow you to demonstrate some of the skills and capabilities you will have acquired.

The following screenshot shows some of the features you will be using:

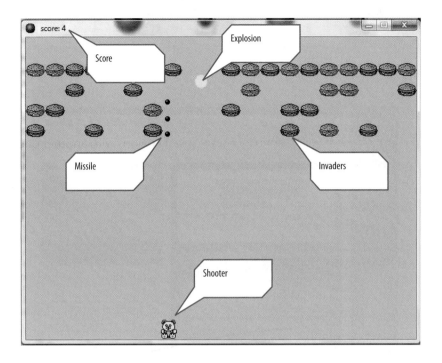

Figure Intro.1

This book also helps you to develop your Functional Skills in ICT. This is all about you being able to use your software skills in the way that best suits the activity that you have been given – in other words, *why* you are doing something in the way that you have chosen. For example, you always need to be thinking about the purpose of what you are doing – what has it got to do with the task, what kind of impact do you want to achieve, who is going to see or use what you're working on i.e. who is your audience, and what is the background of the situation – for example, do you need to produce a formal or informal document? By considering all of these things you should be able to produce the right kind of documents that are 'fit for purpose', i.e. they do the job they need to do. A lot to take in at once I know, but have a look at the Functional Skills tabs as you work through the book and they'll show you what all this means in practice… so that you can use them to help you with your project.

Before we start with Task 1, though, the next few pages show you some of the most important skills that you'll need throughout your whole project – how to download and install the program and resources, start the program, create new files, and save your work. Remember you can return to these pages to remind yourself of these skills if you forget later on in the project.

DOWNLOADING AND INSTALLING THE PROGRAM

The program can be downloaded from the website **http://www.yoyogames.com/**. You will see the home page:

Figure Intro.2

 Select the **MAKE** button and then click on **Download Game Maker**.

 Click on **Download** again.

 Scroll to the bottom of the page and click on **DOWNLOAD GAMEMAKER? HERE**.

 If you get a message warning you about downloading the file click on the **Close** button, then right click on the information bar and select **Download File**.

 Now select **Save** from the dialogue box that you will be shown and save the file in a suitable folder on your computer.

A dialogue box will show you the progress of your download.

 To install the program, double click the gmaker file you have just downloaded and select **Next**.

 Continue through the next screens and eventually select the **Start** button.

 When the program is installed, click on the **Exit** button.

The program will load as shown in Figure Intro.3.

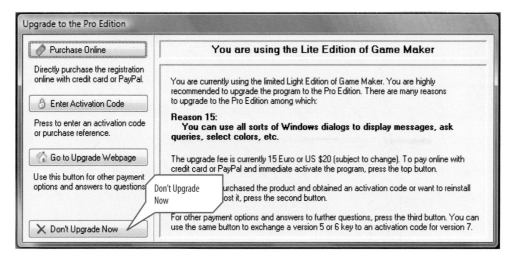

Figure Intro.3

 Select the **Don't Upgrade Now** button.

You should be asked if you want to enable Advanced Mode. Select **Yes**.

 Select the **File** menu and check that **Advanced Mode** is enabled.

STARTING THE PROGRAM

Either:

 Go to **Start** and **All Programs**.

 Select the **Game Maker 7** program group and then **Game Maker**.

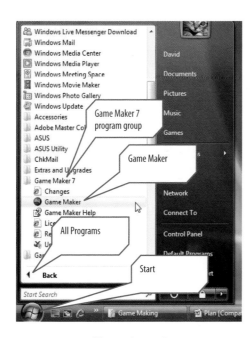

Figure Intro.4

Or:

3 Select the **Game Maker** shortcut on the desktop.

4 Click on **Don't Upgrade Now** (see Figure Intro.3).

5 Ensure that **File** > **Advanced Mode** is ticked as shown in **Figure Intro.5**.

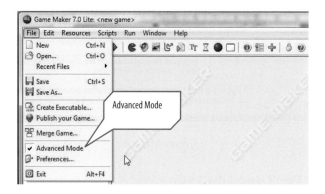

Figure Intro.5

The Game Maker window can be resized just like any other program. When you start creating games it is best to maximise it.

The most important parts of the interface are the folders at the left of the screen, where all the game items are stored, and the toolbar at the top, which has icons for creating the game items and saving and opening the game files.

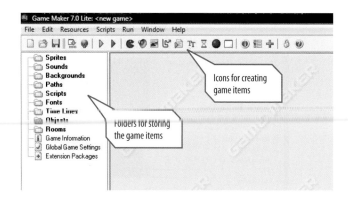

Figure Intro.6

If you place your mouse pointer over icons on the toolbar, a label will appear explaining what it is for.

CREATING A NEW FILE AND SAVING A FILE

 To create a new file, either click on **File** > **New** or use the **Create a New Game** icon on the toolbar.

 To save a file, either use **File** > **Save** (or **Save As...**), or use the **Save the Game** icon on the toolbar.

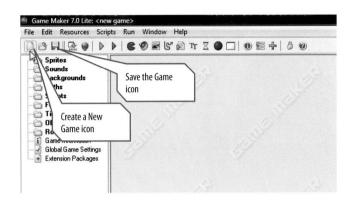

Figure Intro.7

PUBLISHING THE GAME

When you have completed a game, you can create an executable (.exe) file that anyone will be able to run on their computer, so your friends will be able to play your games – even if they do not have Game Maker.

 Either use **File** > **Create Executable** or use the **Create a stand-alone executable for your game** icon on the toolbar.

Figure Intro.8

There is also a menu item and icon for publishing your games on YoYo's website.

Task 1

CREATING A BREAKOUT GAME

TASK BRIEF

The company has sent you an email with the following brief:

From: Big Games Ltd

To: The Game Design Studio

BACKGROUND

Big Games Ltd has identified the need for a Breakout game aimed at new players between the ages of six and ten. It should be simple to play but allow the users to develop their skills in moving a bat around the screen and hitting a ball against the walls and barriers.

TASK REQUIREMENTS

 1   The player should be able to move the bat to the left and right using the cursor keys.

 2   The player should be able to hit the ball against the walls and the barriers.

 3   The barriers should disappear when they are hit by the ball.

 4   There should be an exit for the ball at the top of the screen.

 5   The player should gain a point for every barrier that they hit.

 6   The score should be displayed at the top of the screen.

We invite The Game Design Studio to create a game meeting the above requirements.

As you create the game to meet the requirements, you will cover the following:

SOFTWARE SKILLS

You will:

> Become familiar with the items that make up a computer game
> Be able to create sprites and objects
> Be able to create a room and position the objects in it
> Be able to create events and actions for the objects
> Be able to keep the score and display it on the screen

FUNCTIONAL SKILLS

As you work through this task the Functional Skills tabs will explain to you why the task tackles the brief in the way shown here and explain why you would choose to:

> Organise documents
> Plan the work
> Match the work to the task requirements
> Review work
> Modify your work

CAPABILITY

You will show that you can:

> Design a game to meet the set requirements
> Design the rules for the objects in the game
> Program events and actions so that the objects behave according to the rules

VOCABULARY

You should learn these new words and understand what they mean:

> Sprite
> Object
> Room
> Events
> Actions

RESOURCES

There are two files that show what should be achieved by the end of this task:

Task1.gmk – a Game Maker file that can be used and edited in the program.

Task1.exe – an executable file of the game.

You can download these files from www.payne-gallway.co.uk

Level 3	Level 4	Level 5	Level 6
You have created a new game file	You have saved the file as 'Task1' in the correct folder	You have created actions to keep and display the score	
You have saved the file as 'Task1'	You have created a room, sprites and objects to meet all of the requirements		
You have created a sprite and an object	You have arranged the objects within the room		
	You have created collision events for the ball		

TARGET POINT

Have a look at the following statements before you start your task so you know what you are aiming for.

OK. Let's get started.

Before you start any task, you should organise your area where you are going to save the work.

Create a folder called 'Game Making' and inside it, create a sub-folder called 'Task1' – this is where you will save the file you will be creating in this task.

A FEW IMPORTANT POINTS

Before we begin to create a game, we must understand some of the basic ideas and components of games.

Objects

A game consists of objects. An object could be a ball, a bat, a wall, a character, a gun, a bullet, etc. These objects react with each other during the game.

Sprites

> A sprite is a graphic that represents the object on screen.

> If one of the objects is a ball, then the sprite would be the image of a ball.

> An image of a gun would be used to represent the gun object, etc.

> A sprite is like the clothes worn by the object.

Because the object is represented by an on-screen sprite, it can be changed during the game. For example, if a character gains so many points, they could be represented by a sprite of a different colour.

If an object is a person, they could be represented by a right-facing sprite when they are moving right and a left-facing sprite when they are moving left.

If an object is hit by a bullet, we could change its sprite to an explosion.

We can also use small animations such as animated gif files as sprites.

Events

Things happen to objects during the game and these are called events. The commonest event for an object is a collision when it hits another object, but there are many more.

All objects have a 'creation' event when they first appear. This could be at the start of the game or during it.

Actions

When an object has an event, something happens. This is called an action.

For example, when a ball has a collision event with a wall, the action could be a rebound or movement in the opposite direction, and a sound could be played.

When an object collides with a bullet the action could be to change its sprite to one showing an explosion.

There can be many actions for one event.

Rooms

Rooms are the areas where the game takes place. You can have one room for a game or as many as you want.

An action for an event could be the closing of one room and the opening of another.

You can import backgrounds for the rooms.

STEP 1: DESIGNING THE GAME

Before we begin to create the game, we need to have some basic design ideas.

We need to decide on the objects that we will be using in the game and the sprites that will be used to represent them on screen. We also need to consider the events and actions for each of the objects.

The following table shows the objects that we will need and their events and actions.

Object	Events	Actions
Bat	Cursor keys pressed	Bat moves left or right
Wall	None	None
Barrier	None	None
Ball	Collision with wall	Bounce
	Collision with bat	Move in a random direction
	Collision with barrier	Move in a random direction
		Barrier destroyed
		Score increases by 1

STEP 2: CREATING THE SPRITES

1 Load the program and maximise the window.

The program loads with a new game already present.

2 To create a sprite, either right click on the Sprites folder and select **Create Sprite** as shown in Figure 1.1

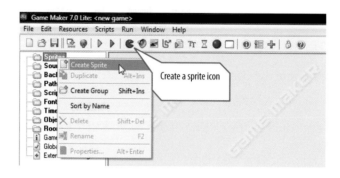

Figure 1.1

or click on the **Create a sprite** icon on the toolbar.

You will be shown the following dialogue box.

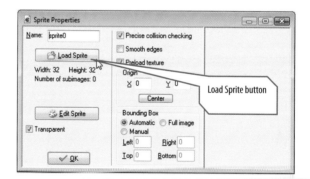

Figure 1.2

3 Click on the **Load Sprite** button and navigate to a folder containing sprites that was installed with the program.

This is the **Game_Maker7\Sprites\various folder**. Select the **Square** sprite by double clicking, as shown in Figure 1.3. We are going to use this sprite for the Wall object.

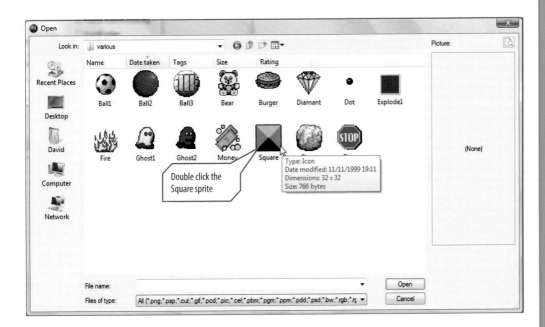

Figure 1.3

 Name this sprite **sprWall** as shown in Figure 1.4.

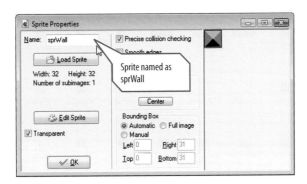

Figure 1.4

It is a good idea to start all of the sprite names with the letters spr to help you remember that they are sprites.

Leave all of the other settings and click on **OK**.

The sprite that we have just created should be shown in the **Sprite** folder at the left of the screen.

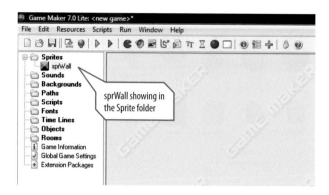

Figure 1.5

Click on the **Create a sprite** icon again. This time we will load a sprite for the ball.

Select **ball2** from the **Game_Maker7\Sprites\breakout** folder as shown in Figure 1.6.

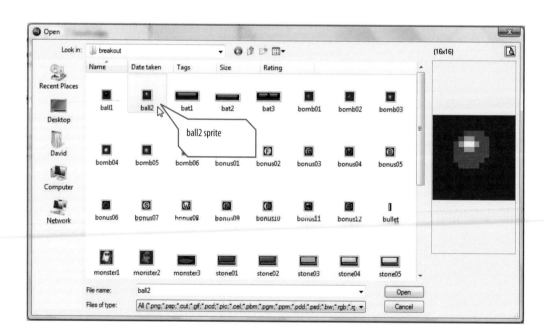

Figure 1.6

Name this sprite as **sprBall** and click on **OK** to save it.

It should appear in the **Sprite** folder, like **sprWall**.

We must now create sprites for the bat and the barrier.

Create them in the same way as the wall and ball sprites but use the following sprites:

⟩ For **sprBat** use **bat1** from the **Game_Maker7\Sprites\breakout** folder.

⟩ For **sprBarrier** use **stone02** from the **Game_Maker7\Sprites\breakout** folder.

The **Sprites** folder should now show all four sprites as shown in Figure 1.7.

Figure 1.7

Well done! That's the first part of the game completed.

Now that we have created the sprites, we can create the objects.

STEP 3: CREATING THE OBJECTS

To create an object either right click on the **Objects** folder and select **Create Object**

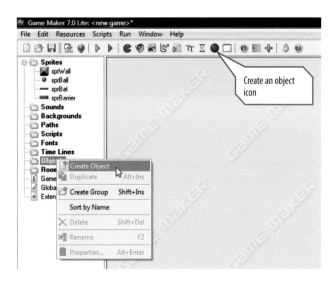

Figure 1.8

or click on the **Create an object** icon on the toolbar.

Name the object **objWall**, click on the **Browse** icon and select **sprWall** as the sprite to represent this object.

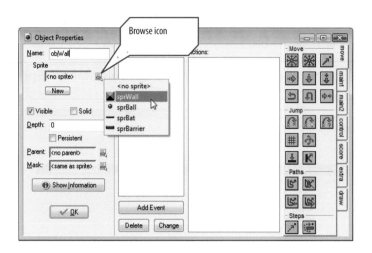

Figure 1.9

This sprite will now be shown in **Sprite** field as shown in Figure 1.10.

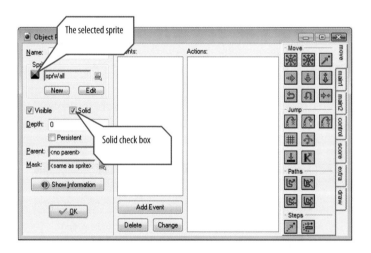

Figure 1.10

Click in the **Solid** check box and then click on **OK**.

Follow items 1 and 2 above to create the following objects:

> objBall using sprBall

> objBat using sprBat

> objBarrier using sprBarrier

The **Objects** folder at the left should show the objects we have just created as shown in Figure 1.11.

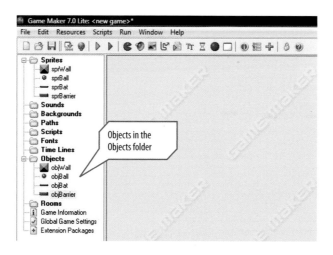

Figure 1.11

Now that the objects have been created, we can create a room and then arrange them in it.

STEP 4: CREATING THE ROOM

To create a room, either right click on the **Rooms** folder and select **Create Room**, or click on the **Create a room** icon on the toolbar.

Figure 1.12

You will now see the room in a new window.

We now have to arrange the objects in the room.

Maximise the window so that all of the room can be seen.

The room has a grid to allow us to arrange the objects more accurately.

The first object we will place in the room is the **objWall**.

We will have to place many instances of this object around the outside.

3 Ensure that the **Objects** tab is selected and select **objWall** as shown in Figure 1.18.

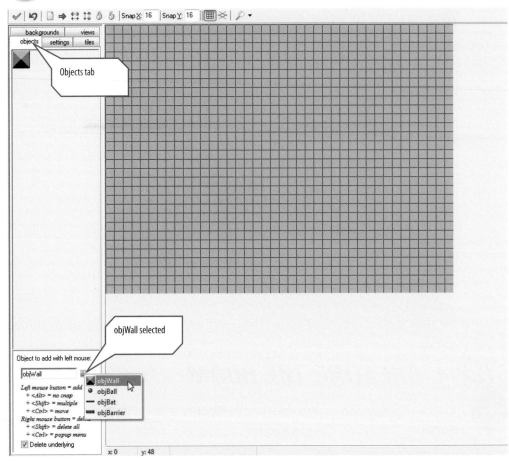

Figure 1.13

 4 Left click around the edges of the room to insert instances of the **objWall** object as shown in **Figure 1.14**.

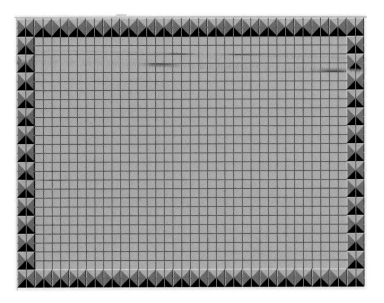

Figure 1.14

Don't worry if you make a mistake – you can right click on an instance of the object to remove it.

We need to do that now to create an exit at the top.

 Remove four instances of the **objWall** object from the centre of the top wall by right clicking.

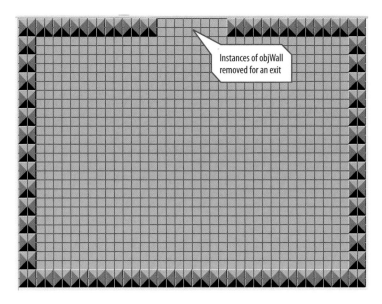

Instances of objWall removed for an exit

Figure 1.15

We must now arrange the barriers in the room.

 Select the **objBarrier** object and left click to insert **fifty** instances of this object at the top of the room.

We need to know exactly how many we are inserting so that when we keep the score, we will know when they have all been destroyed.

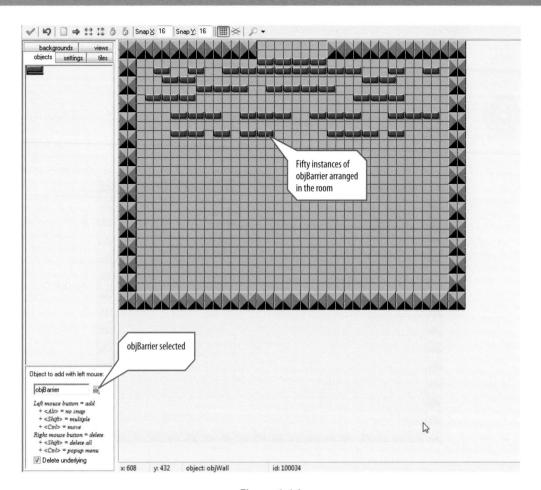

Figure 1.16

Now select **objBat** and place it in the centre of the room, about three-quarters of the way down, and place **objBall** between the lowest barrier and the bat as shown in Figure 1.17.

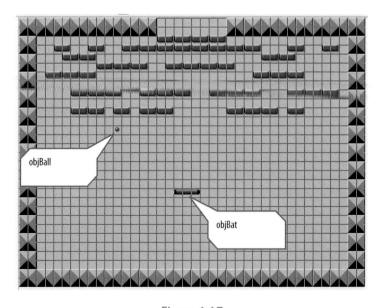

Figure 1.17

It would be a good idea to save the game in case anything goes wrong.

 8 Save the game as **Task1** in the **Task1** folder.

Well done! All the objects have been created and instances of them have been arranged in the room.

Now we have to program the events and actions in accordance with the rules of the game.

STEP 5: PROGRAMMING THE EVENTS AND ACTIONS

We now have to program the events and actions in accordance with the rules of our game.

These are the rules:

> When the left cursor key is pressed, the bat should move to the left.

> When the right cursor key is pressed, the bat should move to the right.

> When the ball hits the wall, it should bounce.

> When the ball hits the bat, it should rebound in a random direction.

> When the ball hits a barrier, it should rebound in a random direction.

> When the ball hits a barrier, it should be destroyed.

> When the ball hits a barrier the score should increase by one.

> The only objects that have events and actions are the bat and the ball.

We will start with the bat.

 1 Double click **objBat** in the **Objects** list at the left.

A window will open, allowing us to set events and actions for this object.

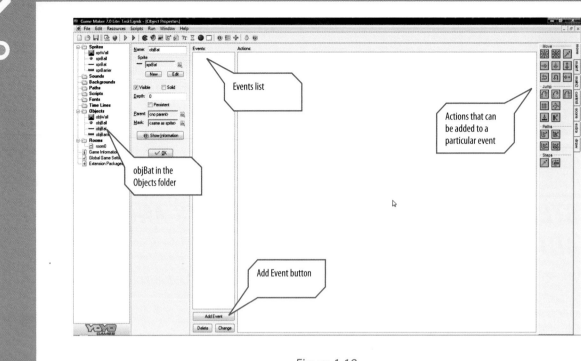

Figure 1.18

SOFTWARE SKILLS
Adding events

2 Click on the **Add Event** button and select **Keyboard** > **<Left>**.

Figure 1.19

This event will now appear at the top of the **Events** list.

We must now make the bat move to the left as the action for this event.

SOFTWARE SKILLS
Adding fixed movement

3 Drag the **Move Fixed** icon into the **Actions** window.

A new window will open allowing us to program the movement.

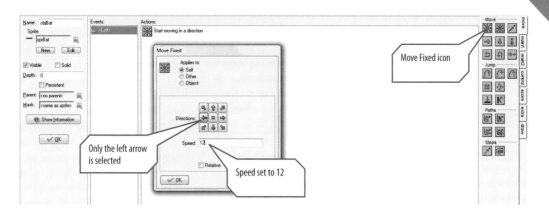

Figure 1.20

 Set the speed to 12 and select only the left arrow, so that the movements will always be to the left, and then click on **OK**.

 Click on **Add Event** and select **Keyboard** > **<Right>**.

This event will be added to the **Events** list and will be the selected event.

 Drag the **Move Fixed** icon into the **Actions** window and set the speed to 12.

Select only the right arrow so that the movements will always be to the right and then click on **OK**.

 Finally click on **OK** to close the **objBat** window.

Let's test our first programmed event!

We will run the game in debug mode so that we will be told of any errors and given help.

 Click on the **Run game in debug mode** icon.

Figure 1.21

The program will save the executable and the game will run.

 Press the left cursor key and then the right one.

The bat should move left and then right.

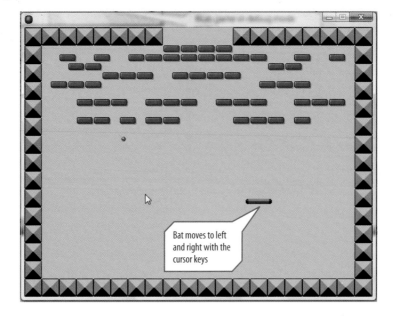

Figure 1.22

The programming works but there is one serious problem!

The bat keeps moving when we stop pressing a cursor key and it goes right out of the room!

We must tell the bat to stop moving when a key isn't being pressed.

 Close the game either by pressing the **Esc** key or by clicking on the **Close window** icon.

 Double click the **objBat** object to open its properties window and select **Add Event**.

 Add the **Key Release** > **<Any key>** event.

This event is the release of any key, including the cursor keys.

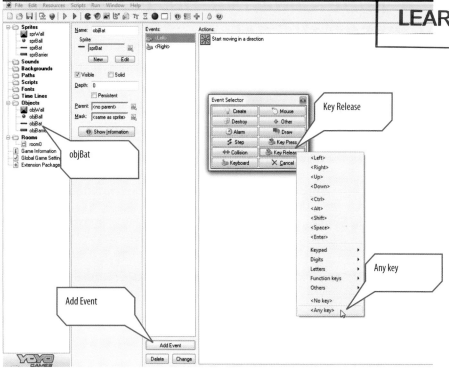

Figure 1.23

When a key is released we want to stop the bat moving to the left or right.

We want to stop its horizontal motion or set its speed to zero.

13   Drag in the **Speed Horizontal** icon from the **Actions** window at the right.

14   Make sure the speed is set at zero and click on **OK**.

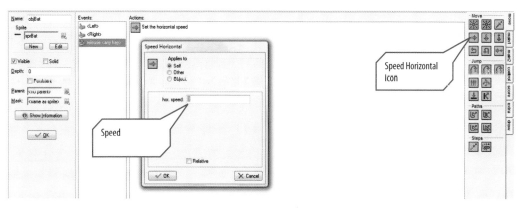

Figure 1.24

15   Click on **OK** to close the **objBat** window and then use the **Run game in debug mode** icon to test the game again.

Congratulations! It works. When you stop pressing a cursor key, the bat stops.

Now we have to program the events and actions for the ball.

STEP 6: PROGRAMMING THE EVENTS AND ACTIONS FOR THE BALL

The main event for the ball is its **Collision** event. We will have to set events for collisions with the wall, the bat and the barriers.

One of the requirements was for the game to display the score and for it to increase every time a barrier is destroyed. We will therefore also use the **Creation** event of the ball to set the score to zero and have it displayed at the top of the window.

 Double click the **objBall** icon to display its properties window.

Click on **Add Event** and select **Create**. The create event for **objBall** will occur once – when the game starts.

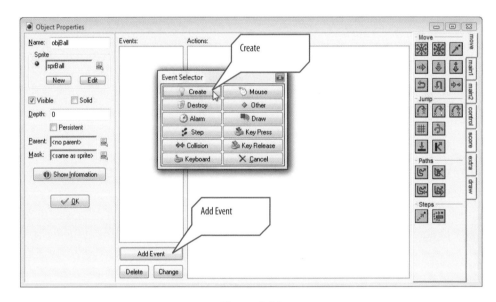

Figure 1.25

 Click on the **Score** tab and drag in the **Set Score** icon, as shown in Figure 1.26.

 Leave the score set at zero and click on **OK**.

 Now drag in the **Score Caption** icon.

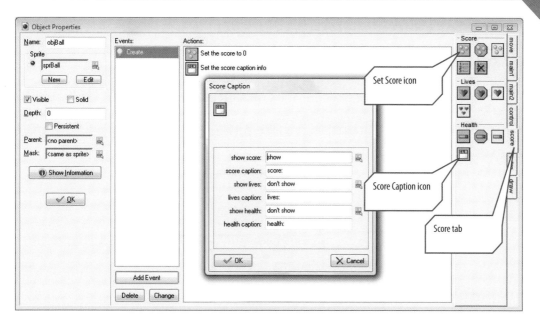

Figure 1.26

Leave the default settings, which will show the score but not the lives or health, and click on **OK**.

When the game is run, the score will appear at the top of the window.

We also need to make the ball move downwards when it is created at the start of the game.

Click on the **Move** tab and drag in the **Move Fixed** icon.

Set the motion to downwards in all of the three directions, so that it doesn't just move straight down. Select a speed of 8 and then click on **OK**.

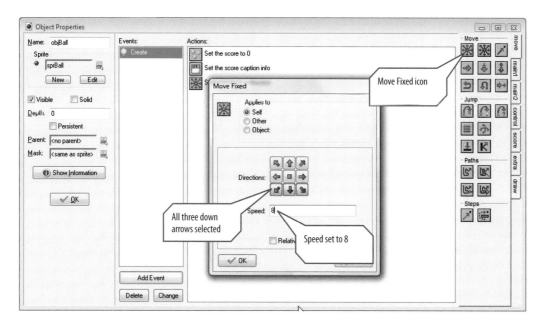

Figure 1.27

We can now start programming the collision events.

SOFTWARE SKILLS
Adding the Collision event

6 Make sure the **objBall** properties window is still open.

Select **Add Event** and click on the **Collision** button.

Select **objWall** as the object to collide with.

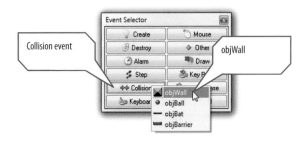

Figure 1.28

The 'collision with objWall' event will now be shown in the **Events** list and will be the selected event.

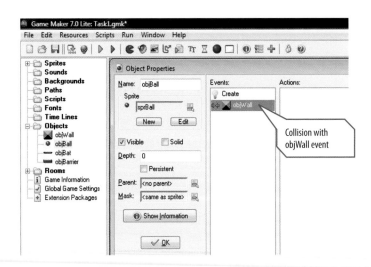

Figure 1.29

When the ball collides with the wall, we want it to rebound or bounce.

SOFTWARE SKILLS
Adding the Bounce action

7 Drag the **Bounce** icon into the **Actions** pane, as shown in Figure 1.30.

Leave the default settings so that the bounce will be more random and click on **OK**.

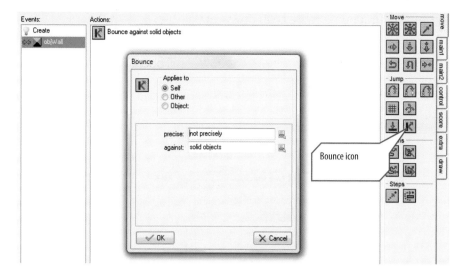

Figure 1.30

 8 Now select **Add Event**, click on **Collision** and select **objBat**.

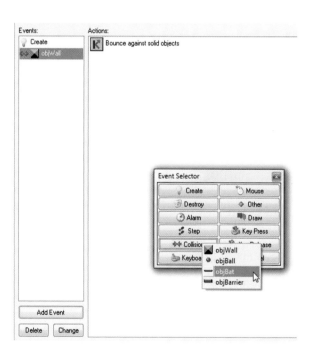

Figure 1.31

The 'collision with objBat' event will now be shown in the **Events** list and will be the selected event.

We want **objBall** to move in a random direction when it collides with the bat. It should move upwards if it hits the top of the bat and downwards if it hits the bottom of the bat.

 9 Drag in the **Move Fixed** icon.

Highlight all of the upward and downward arrows and set the speed to 8.

Finally, click on **OK**.

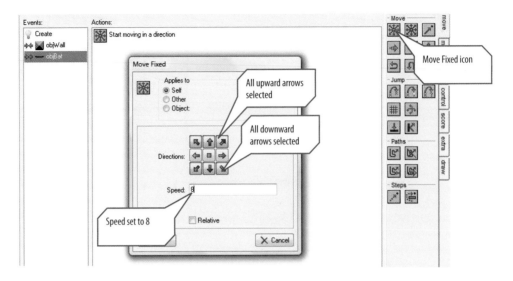

Figure 1.32

We now want to set the events for collision with a barrier. For this collision event we need to program more actions:

> The ball should move downwards in a random direction.

> The barrier should be destroyed.

> The score should increase by 1.

 Now select **Add Event**, click on **Collision** and select **objBarrier**.

 Drag in the **Move Fixed** icon.

Select all of the downward arrows.

Set the speed to 8.

Click on **OK**.

We must now create another action for this event to destroy the barrier after the collision.

SOFTWARE SKILLS
Adding the Destroy Instance action

 Select the **Main1** tab and drag in the **Destroy Instance** icon, as shown in Figure 1.33.

Select the **Other** option so that the barrier will be destroyed and not the ball.

Finally click on OK.

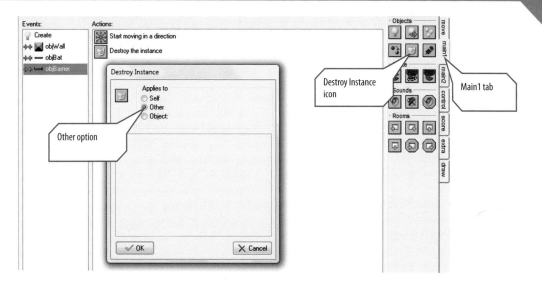

Figure 1.33

This collision event needs one final action – the score must be increased by 1.

 Select the **Score** tab and drag in the **Set Score** icon.

Enter **1** as the new score. Click in the **Relative** box so that 1 will be added to the existing score rather than just replacing it.

If the relative box was not ticked, the score would always be 1!

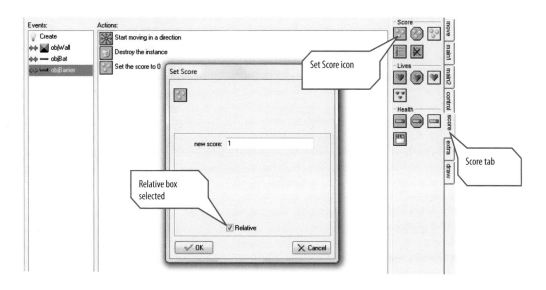

Figure 1.34

Click on **OK**.

 Click on **OK** to close the **objBall** properties window.

We have now programmed events and actions for the bat and the ball.

That should be all that we need, so let's test the game.

 Click on the **Run game in debug mode** icon on the toolbar and test out all of the actions:

> Does the ball move down at the start of the game?

> Does the ball bounce off the walls?

> Are the barriers destroyed after a collision with the ball?

> Does the score increase when a barrier is hit?

Congratulations! It is working as expected!

But – there is always a 'but' – the collision of the ball with the bat is not working correctly. Sometimes it appears to move through it after the collision.

We will have to edit the bat.

 Double click on the **objBat** object to open its properties window.

Click in the **Solid** box as shown in Figure 1.35 and then click on **OK**.

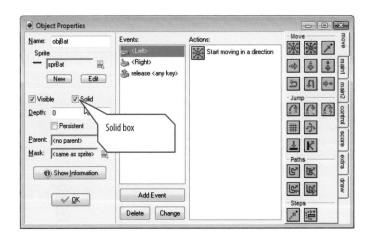

Figure 1.35

Test the game again.

It works far better now!

 Save the competed game and create an executable. For help see page 9.

STEP 7: EVALUATING THE GAME

We can now evaluate our game against the requirements supplied by Big Games Ltd.

They requested the following:

- The player should be able to move the bat to the left and right using the cursor keys.

- The player should be able to hit the ball against the walls and the barriers.

- The barriers should disappear when they are hit by the ball.

- There should be an exit for the ball at the top of the screen.

- The player should gain a point for every barrier that they hit.

- The score should be displayed at the top of the screen.

Our game meets all of these requirements. Well done!

Although the game meets all of the original requirements, we should always think of ways to improve it. The three most obvious items that need improving are:

- The bat moves through the wall. It should stop when it hits the wall.

- When the ball moves through the exit, a message should appear saying that the player has won the game and asking them if they want to play again.

- There is no sound.

You should be able to think of several more. Whatever project you are working on, you should be able to suggest ways in which it could be improved.

CHECKPOINT

Check that you can:

- Explain what is meant by a sprite, object, room, event and action

- Create sprites and objects

- Create a room and position the objects in it

- Create events and actions for the objects

- Keep the score and display it on the screen

ASSESSMENT POINT

Now let's assess the work. Look back at the table at the beginning of this section (**Target point**) and decide on which of the statements you can answer 'Yes' to.

Did you do as well as you expected? Could you improve your work? Add a comment to your work to show what you could do to improve it so that next time you'll remember to do it the first time.

Task 2

IMPROVING THE BREAKOUT GAME

TASK BRIEF

The company likes your game and has sent you an email with some suggested improvements that they would like you to make:

From: Big Games Ltd

To: The Game Design Studio

BACKGROUND

Big Games Ltd has evaluated your initial game design and would like you to develop it with the following new requirements.

TASK REQUIREMENTS

 1 There should be an initial splash screen with the name of the game and some instructions for the players.

 2 There should be sounds when the ball hits the walls, the bat and the barriers.

 3 The bat should stop moving when it hits a wall.

 4 The player should lose a point if the ball falls below the bat.

 5 There should be another exit at the bottom of the screen and if the ball falls through it, the player loses the game.

 6 Messages should be displayed telling the player that they have won or lost the game.

 7 The player should be able to restart the game.

We invite The Game Design Studio to develop their game to meet these extra requirements.

As you improve the game to meet these new requirements, you will cover the following:

SOFTWARE SKILLS

You will be able to:

> Create and add a background to a page
> Create an action to move from one page to another
> Add sounds to collision events
> Check the position of the ball so that points can be deducted if it falls below the bat
> Change the horizontal speed of an object
> Create invisible objects
> Display messages
> Create an event to restart the game

FUNCTIONAL SKILLS

As you work through this task, the Functional Skills tabs will explain to you why the task tackles the brief in the way shown here and explain why you would choose to:

> Create a room background
> Combine images and sounds
> Recognise copyright
> Give messages to the player
> Review work

CAPABILITY

You will show that you can:

> Act on feedback to edit and refine the game
> Design complex rules for the objects in the game
> Combine graphics, text and sound
> Create a series of control actions

VOCABULARY

You should learn this new word and understand what it means:

> Splash screen

Level 3	Level 4	Level 5	Level 6
You have copied the 'Task1' file into the new folder and renamed it as 'Task2'	You have created an object, without a sprite, with an action to move from one room to another	You have added an action to check the position of the ball when it collides with the wall	You have added an action to deduct a point if the ball is below a certain level
You have created a new room and added a background	You have added sounds to the collision events		
	You have created actions to display messages		
	You have added invisible objects		

TARGET POINT

Have a look at the following statements before you start your task so you know what you are aiming for.

OK. Let's get started.

Before you start any task, you should organise your area where you are going to save the work.

Create a folder called 'Task2' inside the Game Making folder – this is where you will save the file you will be creating in this task.

Copy Task1.gmk from the Task1 folder into the Task2 folder and rename it as 'Task2.gmk'. Make sure that you copy the *.gmk* file, because there should also be a file called 'Task1.gb1'. This is a backup file that was created the last time you edited the Task1 game.

STEP 1: CREATING A NEW ROOM WITH A BACKGROUND

The first requirement is for us to add a splash screen.

This means that we have to add a new room and it should be the first to load – that means it will have to come before the existing one.

We will program it to move to the next room when the space bar is pressed.

 Open **Task2** and create a new room. We have already covered this on page 19.

The first room we created was automatically named as **room0**, so the new one is **room1**.

The first thing we will do is rename the rooms.

To rename the room, either use the normal Windows method of selecting it and then clicking on the name again or right clicking on it and selecting **Rename** from the menu.

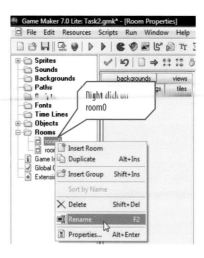

Figure 2.1

 Rename **room0** as 'Game' and **room1** as 'Splash'.

We need to move the Splash room above the Game room so that it appears first when the game is run. This can be done by dragging it.

 3 Drag the **Splash** room so that it is above the **Game** room as shown in Figure 2.2.

Figure 2.2

 4 Make sure that the **Splash** room is selected and then maximise its window.

We now have to create a graphic in a graphics program that can be imported into Game Maker and added as a background to the page. We have to create the graphic so that it is the exact size of the page we are importing it into.

You will probably have noticed that there is a grid on the page and that the coordinates of each cell of the grid are displayed at the bottom of the window.

If you point to the cell at the left of the top row, the coordinates are X: 0 and Y:0 as shown in Figure 2.3.

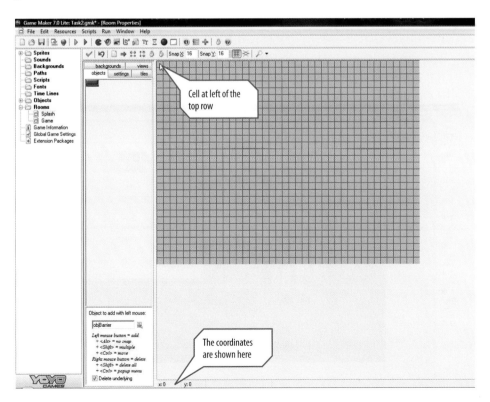

Figure 2.3

Look at the coordinates of other cells and you should see that the X coordinates increase as you move to the right and the Y coordinates increase as you move down the grid.

The coordinates for the last cell at the right of the bottom row are X: 624 and Y: 464.

The units are in pixels and so the image should have a size of 624 × 464 pixels. The following screen print shows how to set the image size in Adobe Fireworks CS3.

 5 Select **Create New** > **Fireworks Document**.

 6 Set the image size to 624 × 464 pixels.

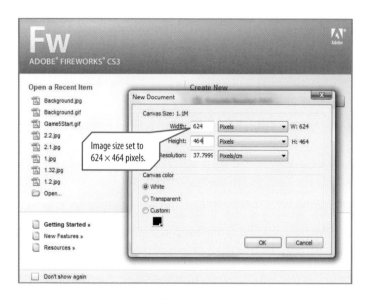

Figure 2.4

You could open a digital image in Fireworks using **File** > **Open**.

You can adjust its size by using **Modify menu** > **Canvas** > **Image size** and then adjusting the size as near as you can to 624 × 464 pixels.

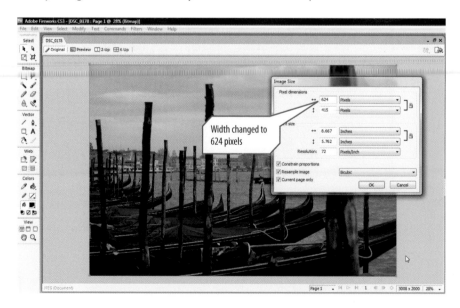

Figure 2.5

You can now create a background for the splash room. It should show the name of the game and instructions for the players. You could also add your name as the programmer.

A simple design is shown in Figure 2.6 but you should be able to create something far better!

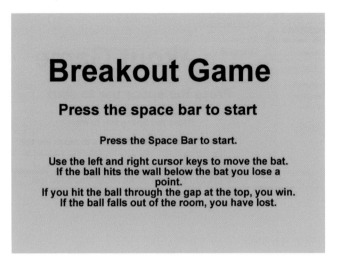

Figure 2.6

You should save the image as a jpeg (.jpg) file, as this reduces the file size and makes it quicker to load.

We now have to import this graphic as a background for the room.

 Either right click on the **Backgrounds** folder at the left and select **Create Background** or click on the **Create a background** icon on the toolbar.

 Click on **Load Background**, navigate to the folder containing your graphic, select it and click on **Open**.

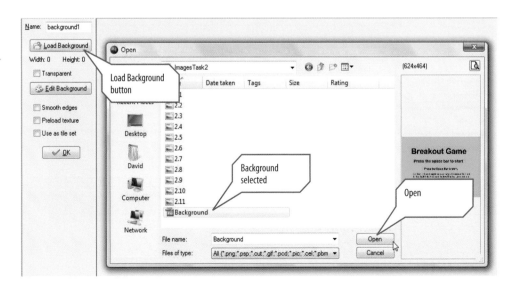

Figure 2.7

The program automatically gives the file a number, starting with 0, but you can edit the name of the file by typing over the text in the name box and clicking on **OK**. In this example it has been renamed as **background1**.

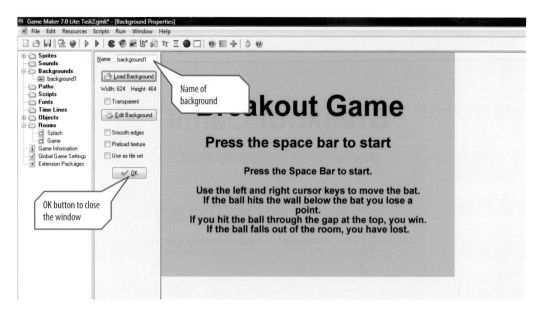

Figure 2.8

We now have to import this background onto the splash page.

SOFTWARE SKILLS
Adding a background to a page

(9) Click on the **Background tab** of the splash page properties window and select the file **background1** (or whatever you renamed it as).

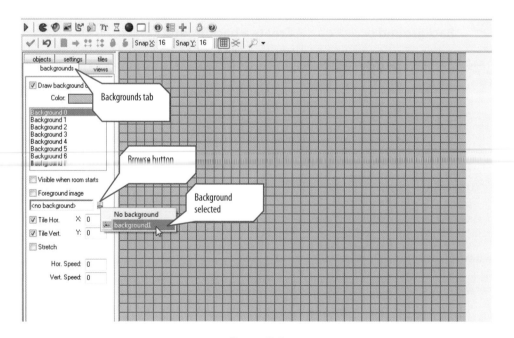

Figure 2.9

(10) The selected background will appear in the room.

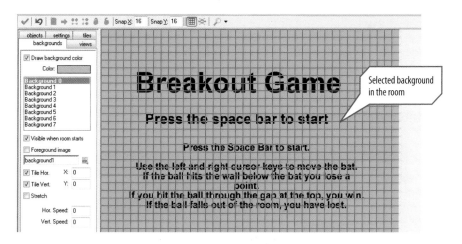

Figure 2.10

The instructions given on our splash page say that the game begins by pressing the space bar, so now we must create a new object that will open the **Game** page when the space bar is pressed.

11 Either right click on the **Objects** folder or click the **Create an object** icon on the toolbar.

12 Name the object as **objControl** but do not add a sprite.

13 Click on **Add Event** and select **Keyboard** > **<Space>**.

14 To select the action for this event, click on the **Main1** tab and drag in the **Next Room** icon.

You can select a transition from the list.

SOFTWARE SKILLS
Adding a control object

SOFTWARE SKILLS
Adding an action to move to next room

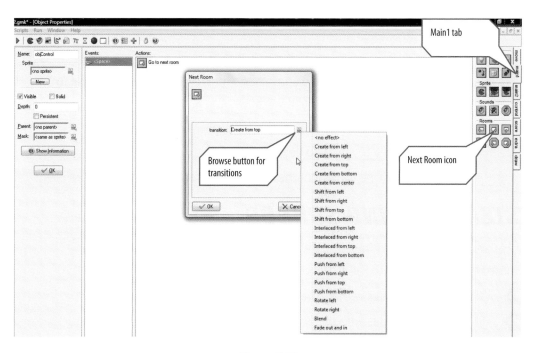

Figure 2.11

 15 Click on **OK** to close the object's properties window.

We must now add this object to the **Splash** room. (Because we did not add a sprite to the object, it will not be seen when the game is run).

16 Click on the **Objects** tab of the room's properties window and then select **objControl** from the list.

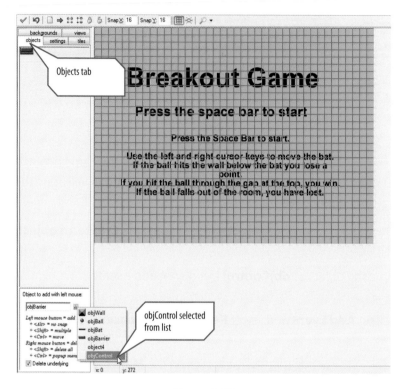

Figure 2.12

 17 Now click somewhere on the page to place this object.

It will be shown as a question mark inside a blue circle because it does not have a sprite.

18 Save the game again before we test it and then click on the **Run game in debug mode** icon to test that it works.

Press the **space bar** and yes! It works. Well done.

Press the **Esc** key to return to design mode.

We have now done the first of the new requirements given to us by our client.

STEP 2: ADDING SOUNDS

The next requirement given to us in our brief was to add sounds.

These need to be added to the ball's collision events. There are three of these:

➤ When the ball collides with the bat.

➤ When the ball collides with the wall.

➤ When the ball collides with the barriers.

We can add the sounds directly to each collision event but it's a good idea to select the sounds first so we can test them out.

 Either right click on the **Sounds** folder and select **Create Sound** or click on the **Create a sound** icon on the toolbar.

 Click on **Load Sound**, navigate to the **Game_Maker7\Sounds** folder and select a sound. The file **zap** has been chosen in this example, but you might prefer another sound. Remember to make it appropriate for how it is being used and for your audience.

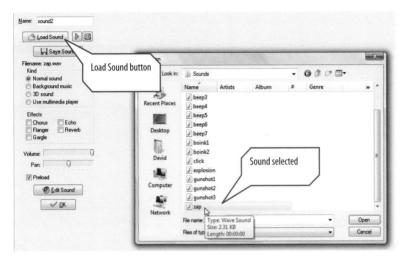

Figure 2.13

You could also load a sound if you have created any or downloaded copyright-free ones from the Internet.

 Click on the **Play the Sound** icon to listen to this sound you have chosen.

Click on the **Stop the Sound** icon to stop it because it will keep repeating itself.

You can change the sound by adding effects to it to create different versions of the same sound as shown in Figure 2.14.When you have created a sound you like, rename it by typing a new name in the name box and click on **OK**.

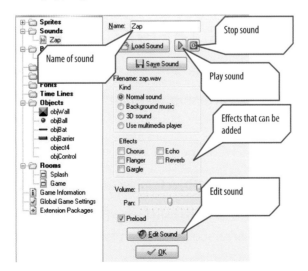

Figure 2.14

Repeat items 1 to 3 until you have created and saved three different sounds.

We now have to add these sounds to the ball's three collision events.

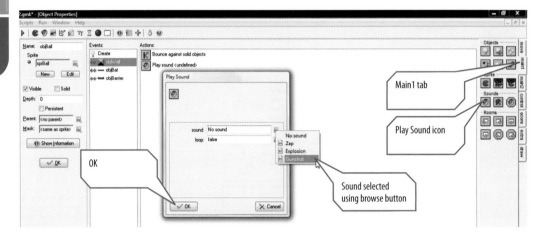 Double click the object called **objBall** in the Objects folder to open its properties window and select **Collision event with object objWall** by clicking on it.

To add a sound action to this event, click on the **Main1** tab and drag in the **Play Sound** icon.

Select one of the sounds you have just created from the list and click on **OK**.

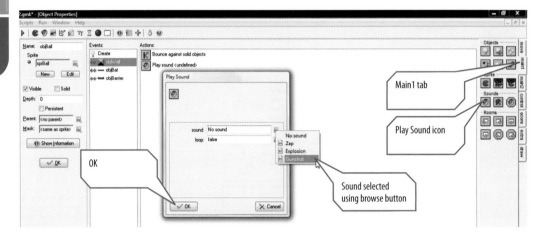

Figure 2.15

Add a sound for each of the collision events by selecting them in turn.

Finally, click on **OK** to close the **objBall** properties window.

 Save the game again and test it by clicking on the **Run game in debug mode** icon to check that the three different sounds play for the collision events.

That's another of the client's requirements met.

STEP 3: STOPPING THE BAT WHEN IT HITS THE WALL

The next requirement is for the bat to stop when it hits a wall so it doesn't keep going out of the room.

This should be easy for us now we are getting used to the program.

 Double click **objBat** in the **Objects** folder to open its properties window.

We will have to add a collision event for the bat so that when it collides with the wall object, its horizontal speed will be set to zero – i.e. it will stop.

We did a similar action with the **Key Release** event for this object.

2 Click on **Add Event** and select **Collision** > **objWall**.

3 Drag in the **Speed Horizontal** icon, leave the speed set to zero and click on **OK**.

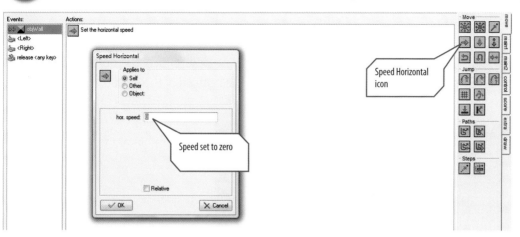

Figure 2.16

4 Click on **OK** to close the **objBat** properties window.

5 Save the game again and test it by clicking on the **Run game in debug mode** icon.

Wow! Yet another thing working correctly!

STEP 4: LOSING A POINT IF THE BALL HITS THE WALL BELOW THE BAT

Our next requirement that we need to meet is making the player lose a point if the ball hits the wall below the bat.

We have already looked at the X and Y coordinates in this task.

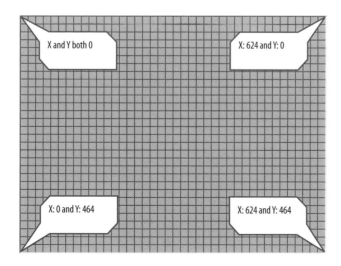

Figure 2.17

To meet this requirement, all the program will be doing is comparing the Y coordinate of the bat with the Y coordinate of the ball when it hits the wall. If the Y coordinate of the ball when it hits the wall is greater than the Y coordinate of the bat, then we will deduct 1 point.

Sounds easy!

 Open the Game room and place the mouse pointer over the object called **objBat** and look at the coordinates at the bottom of the screen.

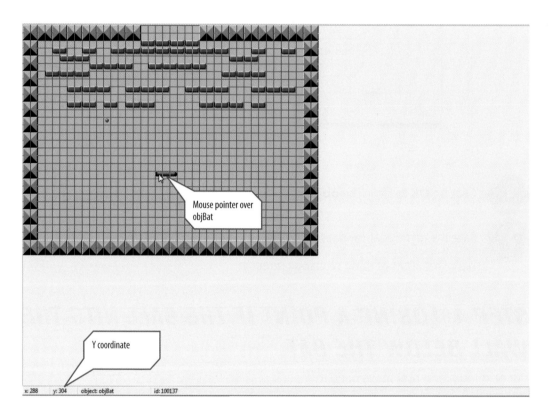

Figure 2.18

In the example above, the Y coordinate is 304 **but in your game it may be different**.

Whenever the ball collides with the **objWall**, we now have to check the Y coordinate.

If it is greater than 304, one point has to be deducted from the score.

 Double click **objBall** in the **Objects** folder to open its properties window.

 Select **Collision event with object objWall** in the Events list.

Here's how we can check the Y coordinate whenever a collision occurs.

>> Select the **Control** tab and drag in the **Test Variable** icon. Enter **y** as the variable to test.

>> Enter the Y coordinate of **objBat** as the value to test – in this case it is 304.

>> Enter **larger than** as the operation.

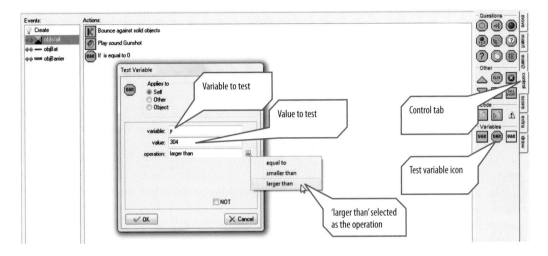

Figure 2.19

>> Click on **OK**.

In the **Actions** window the text next to the **Test Variable** icon should show what you have just entered.

In this case it reads **If y is larger than 304**.

Figure 2.20

We have therefore programmed an IF statement – if the Y co-ordinate is greater than 304, the software knows it has to do something.

Directly under this icon we now have to tell the program what to do if **y** is greater than 304.

 Select the **Score** tab and drag in the **Set Score** icon.

Enter **-1** as the new score and remember to click in the **Relative** box.

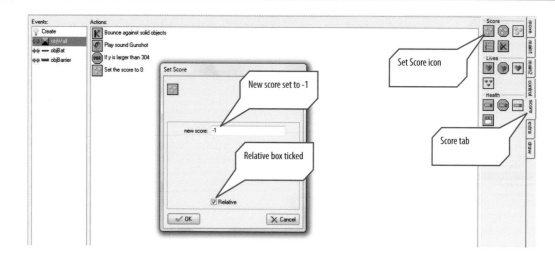

Figure 2.21

 Click on **OK** to close this dialogue box and then on **OK** again to close the **objBall** properties window.

 Save the game again and test it by clicking on the **Run game in debug mode** icon.

Check that the score goes down by 1 every time the ball goes below the bat.

Yes! It works. Well done.

STEP 5: WINNING, LOSING AND RESTARTING THE GAME

We are now going to tackle the last three requirements of the client's brief at the same time.

These are as follows:

> There should be another exit at the bottom of the screen and if the ball falls through it, the player loses the game.

> Messages should be displayed telling the player that they have won or lost the game.

> The player should be able to restart the game.

The first of these requirements is easy to achieve.

 Right click on the **objWall** instances immediately below the bat at the bottom of the screen and remove three instances.

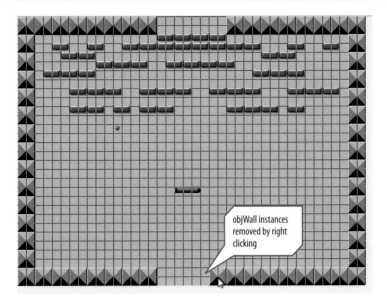

Figure 2.22

The next parts are more difficult. How will the program 'know' if the ball has moved through the exits at the top or the bottom of the screen?

Like most problems, there are different ways of solving it.

Since we can create **invisible** objects, we could:

> Create an invisible wall across the exit at the top of the screen – if the ball collides with it, the player has won.

> Create another invisible wall across the exit at the bottom of the screen – if the ball collides with it, the player has lost.

That would mean creating two new objects.

Or we could create just one invisible object, use it in both exits and check the coordinates when the ball collides with it. So if the Y coordinate is zero, the player has won; if the Y coordinate is 464, the player has lost.

Let's go with the second option.

 Create a new sprite named **sprInvisible** and select **stone09** from the **Game_Maker7\Sprites\breakout** folder.

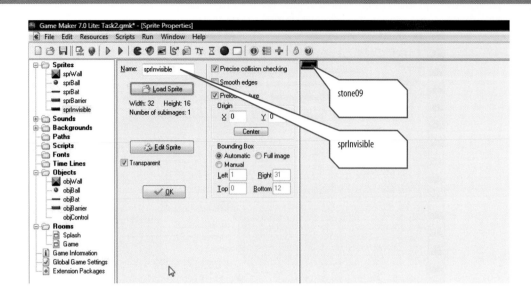

Figure 2.23

3 Click on **OK** to close the properties window.

4 Create a new object called **objInvisible** and select **sprInvisible** as the sprite to represent it on screen.

Click in the **Visible** box to remove the tick.

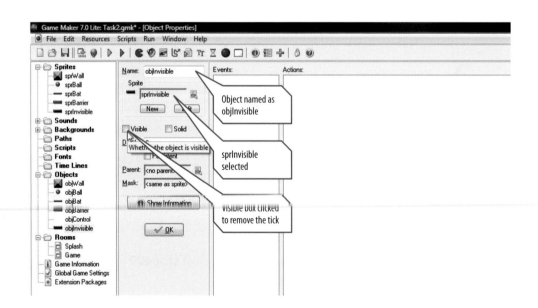

Figure 2.24

This means that when the game is run, the object will not be seen but other objects will still be able to collide with it.

5 Click on **OK** to close the properties window.

6 Select **objInvisible** and add instances of this object in the exits at the top and bottom of the screen as shown in Figure 2.25.

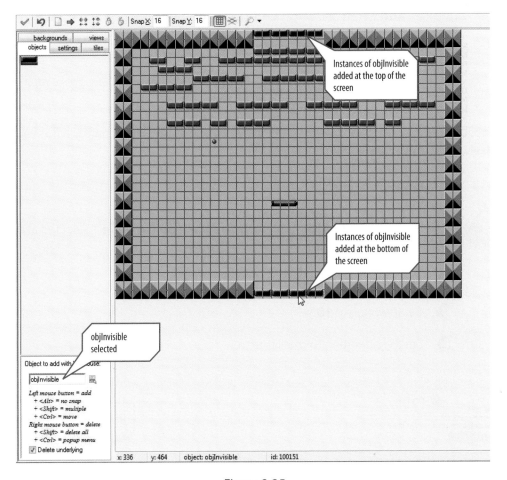

Figure 2.25

Let's think about what we want to happen. We want the program to check the Y coordinates when the ball collides with this object and then tell the player whether they have won or lost. So:

> If the Y coordinate equals zero, a message has to appear saying that the player has won the game and the game restarts.

> If the Y coordinate equals 464, a message has to appear saying that the player has lost the game and the game restarts.

We can write this down as:

> On collision with objInvisible, check the Y coordinate.

> If Y = 0 then display message 'You have won the game'.

> Restart the game.

> Else display message 'You have lost the game'.

> Restart the game.

OK, let's try to program this.

 Double click **objBall** in the **Objects** folder to open its properties window.

Click on **Add Event** and select **Collision** > **objInvisible**.

We now have to program the actions for this event.

We are going to make a slight change because **objInvisible** has a thickness of several pixels and this means that the Y coordinate will never read as 0.

No problem. We can easily solve this. Instead of checking if the Y coordinate is zero, we will check if it is less than ten.

OK. Let's get started.

 Make sure that the **Collision event with object objInvisible** is selected and drag in the **Test Variable** icon from the **Control** tab.

> Set the variable to **y**.

> Set the value to **10**.

> Set the operation to smaller than.

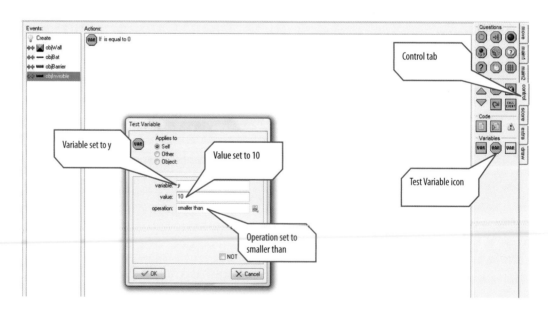

Figure 2.26

Click on **OK**.

We must now state what should happen if the y value is less than ten.

In this case we want a message to appear and then the game to restart.

We therefore need two actions to occur, so we will have to place them in a block.

Drag in the **Start Block** icon as shown in Figure 2.27.

Figure 2.27

Now select the **main2** tab and drag in the **Display Message** icon.

Enter a suitable message saying that the player has won the game and then click on **OK**.

Now drag in the **Restart Game** icon from the **main2** tab and finally the **End Block** icon from the **control** tab.

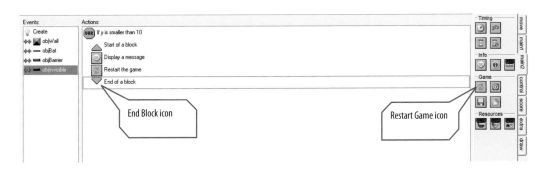

Figure 2.28

We now have to program what will happen if the y coordinate is **not** less than 10.

Drag in the **Else** icon from the **control** tab.

Figure 2.29

13 Now add the following:

➤ The **Start Block** icon.

➤ The **Display Message** icon with a message saying that the player has lost the game.

➤ The **Restart Game** icon.

➤ The **End Block** icon.

The actions for this event should be like those shown in Figure 2.30.

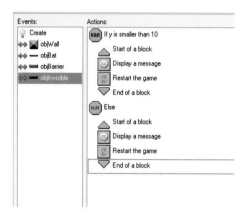

Figure 2.30

Click on **OK** to close the properties window for this event.

We've now completed all the tasks in the client's brief so we could send our game to them. But what if something doesn't work? That wouldn't look good. So let's test it.

STEP 6: TESTING AND EVALUATING THE GAME

 Save the game again and then click on the **Run game in debug mode** icon.

 Test all aspects of the game, especially the messages to check if they are shown when the ball leaves by the exits and then check that the game restarts.

 We must also check that the game meets all of the client's requirements.

Requirement	Met?
There should be an initial splash screen with the name of the game and some instructions for the players.	✓
There should be sounds when the ball hits the walls, the bat and the barriers.	✓
The bat should stop moving when it hits a wall.	✓
The player should lose a point if the ball falls below the bat.	✓
There should be another exit at the bottom of the screen and if the ball falls through it, the player loses the game.	✓
Messages should be displayed telling the player that they have won or lost the game.	✓
The player should be able to restart the game.	✓

Well done! We have met all of the requirements.

 4 Either use **File** > **Create Executable** or use the **Create a stand-alone executable for your game** icon on the toolbar to use the game.

Let's get playing!

CHECKPOINT

Check that you can:

❯ Create and add a background to a page

❯ Create an action to move from one page to another

❯ Add sounds to collision events

❯ Check the position of the ball so that points can be deducted if it falls below the bat

❯ Change the horizontal speed of an object

❯ Create invisible objects

❯ Display messages

❯ Create an event to restart the game

ASSESSMENT POINT

Now let's assess the work. Look back at the table at the beginning of this section (**Target point**) and decide on which of the statements you can answer 'Yes' to.

Did you do as well as you expected? Could you improve your work? Add a comment to your work to show what you could do to improve it so that next time you'll remember to do it the first time.

Task 3

CREATING A PACMAN GAME

TASK BRIEF

The company are really pleased with the Breakout game. They are especially impressed that you incorporated all of their requirements and tested the final game. They have sent you the following email:

From: Big Games Ltd

To: The Game Design Studio

BACKGROUND

Big Games Ltd would like you to submit plans for a Pacman game. This should again be aimed at inexperienced players between the ages of six and ten.

TASK REQUIREMENTS

1. The Pacman character should be able to move in four directions using the cursor keys and always face the way it is moving.

2. At the start of the game, the Pacman should have three lives and lose one if it collides with a monster.

3. When all three lives have been lost, the player should receive a message telling them that they have lost the game and it should then restart.

4. If a monster hits a wall, it should reverse its direction.

5. There should be food items for the Pacman character to eat and the player should gain a point for each item eaten.

6. When the player has gained a certain number of points, they should move to a harder game level.

7. The game should have sound.

We invite The Game Design Studio to create a game to meet these requirements.

As you create the game to meet these requirements, you will use the software skills and capability you developed in the last task and cover the following new ones:

SOFTWARE SKILLS

You will be able to:

> Change the sprite used for an object during the game
> Set and display the number of lives
> Test the number of lives
> Test the score
> Reverse the direction of movement of an object
> Move to a new room when the points reach a certain number

FUNCTIONAL SKILLS

As you work through this task, the Functional Skills tabs will explain to you why the task tackles the brief in the way shown here and explain why you would choose to:

> Design and plan your work
> Select appropriate media files
> Re-use events and actions
> Test and evaluate your work

CAPABILITY

You will show that you can:

> Create a game to meet the requirements
> Select suitable images to be used as sprites
> Select suitable sounds
> Formulate the rules needed for the game
> Program series of events and actions to obey these rules

VOCABULARY

There are no new words used in this task.

RESOURCES

There are two files that show what should be achieved by the end of this task:

Task3.gmk – a Game Maker file that can be used and edited in the program.

Task3.exe – an executable file of the game.

You can download these files from www.payne-gallway.co.uk

TARGET POINT

Have a look at the following statements before you start your task so you know what you are aiming for.

In this task you will be required to make some decisions for yourself as items covered in Tasks 1 and 2 will not be repeated in this task.

Level 3	Level 4	Level 5	Level 6
You have created a new file and saved it as 'Task3' on the 'Task3' folder	You have selected and created suitable sprites for the game	You have added and displayed the number of lives	You have created events to test the number of lives
You have created a new room	You have created objects using the sprites	You have created events to increase the score	You have created events to test the score
You have created sprites	You have arranged the objects within the room	You have created events to decrease the number of lives	Your game meets all of the requirements
You have created objects	You have created events for the movement of the objects	You have created events to display messages	
	You have set and displayed the score	You have created an event to restart the game	

OK. Let's get started.

Before you start any task, you should organise your area where you are going to save the work.

Create a folder called 'Task3' inside the Game Making folder – this is where you will save the file you will be creating in this task.

STEP 1: DESIGNING THE GAME

Before starting to create the game all of the objects, events and actions should be designed.

FUNCTIONAL SKILLS

Plans and designs are important because:

- *They show all of your ideas, so you could easily present them to your client, and they are easy and cheap to change if your client doesn't like them*

- *When the project is under way, you can keep looking back at the documents to make sure you have done everything you needed to*

Object	Events	Actions
Pacman	Right cursor key pressed	Pacman moves to right sprRight used
	Left cursor key pressed	Pacman moves to left sprLeft used
	Up cursor key pressed	Pacman moves up sprUp used
	Down cursor key pressed	Pacman moves down sprDown used
	Creation	Score set to zero Score displayed Lives set to zero Lives displayed
	Collision with wall	Movement stopped
	Collision with food	Score increases by 1 Score variable tested If Score equals 25 then display a message and move to a new level sprFood destroyed
	Collision with monster	Lives decreased by 1 Lives variable tested If Lives equals zero then display a message and restart game
Monsters 1 to 5	Creation	Start moving in a vertical or horizontal direction
	Collision with wall	Direction reversed
	Collision with Pacman	Direction reversed (When a monster collides with the Pacman, we are going to create an action to reverse the direction of the monster – otherwise it would keep colliding with Pacman, who would lose all of its lives at once!)
Food	None	None
Wall	None	None

These objects, events and rules should be all we need to create the game to the requirements given by our clients.

STEP 2: CREATING THE ROOM, SPRITES AND OBJECTS

You have acquired most of the skills for this section in Tasks 1 and 2, so this step will not be covered in great detail.

 Create a new room (see page 19).

 Create your sprites. Load the following graphics and name them as shown in the table below.

Create a new room (see page 19).

Graphic to load	Name of sprite
dot	sprFood
wall	sprWall
monster1	sprMonster1
monster2	sprMonster2
monster3	sprMonster3
monster4	sprMonster4
monster5	sprMonster5
pacman_down	sprDown
pacman_left	sprLeft
pacman_right	sprRight
pacman_up	sprUp

The sprites for this game can be found in the following folder: **Game_Maker7\Sprites\pacman**.

Instructions for creating sprites can be found on page 14.

Your **Sprites** folder should look like that shown in Figure 3.1.

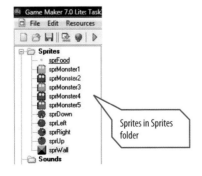

Figure 3.1

FUNCTIONAL SKILLS

Selecting suitable images – we have to consider the objects that the sprite images will be representing in the game so that they are appropriate. It wouldn't be appropriate to represent a monster object with a smiley face sprite image

We must now create some objects using these sprites.

We do not need to create four different Pacman objects. We will create just one using **sprRight**.

 Create the objects as shown in the following table (see page 17).

Object	Sprite
objWall	sprWall
objFood	sprFood
objPacman	sprRight
objMonster1	sprMonster1
objMonster2	sprMonster2
objMonster3	sprMonster3
objMonster4	sprMonster4
objMonster5	sprMonster5

IMPORTANT POINT

Remember to make objWall, objPacman and all of the monsters solid in their properties windows.

We will start by arranging the objects in the room (see page 19).

As most of the sprites used in this game are 32 pixels, we will change the grid size from 16 to 32.

SOFTWARE SKILLS
Changing the grid size

 Change the X and Y grid sizes from 16 to 32 as shown in Figure 3.2.

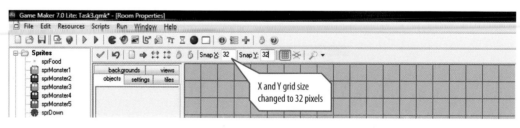

Figure 3.2

 Select **objWall** and create instances of this object around the outside and inside to create a maze (see Figure 3.3).

6 Since we have decided that the player needs 25 points to win the game, arrange 30 instances of **objFood** throughout the room as shown in Figure 3.3.

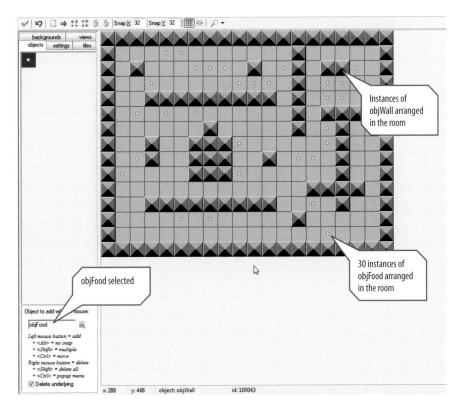

Figure 3.3

7 Now arrange the monsters as shown in Figure 3.4.

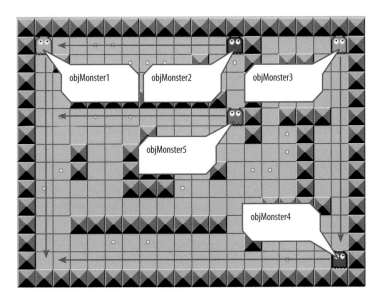

Figure 3.4

It is important that we remember where we have placed each monster as they will be moving in different directions as indicated by the arrows. Monsters 1 and 3 will be moving vertically and Monsters 2, 4 and 5 will be moving horizontally.

All we now have left to do is to arrange **objPacman**.

8 Place **objPacman** in the bottom left-hand corner.

That's it. All of the objects are arranged and we can begin to program the events and actions.

STEP 3: CREATING SOUNDS

In this game we will have sounds for collisions between **objPacman** and:

> objFood.

> objWall.

> objMonster1 to 5.

Load suitable sounds from the **Game_Maker7\Sounds** folder and save them as:

> Food.

> Wall.

> Monster.

See page 44 for instructions on how to load sounds.

STEP 4: PROGRAMMING EVENTS AND ACTIONS

The only objects that need events and actions are the Pacman and Monster objects.

We will start with the Monster objects and we must consider the following:

> When a monster object is created, it must start to move at a certain speed in a horizontal or vertical direction.

> When a monster collides with the wall object, it must reverse its direction.

> When a monster collides with the Pacman object, it must reverse its direction.

Remember: Monsters 1 and 3 will be moving vertically and Monsters 2, 4 and 5 will be moving horizontally. Let's see how we do this.

1 Double click **objMonster1** in the **Objects** folder to open its properties window.

2 **Add Event** > **Create** and drag in the **Move Fixed** icon.

Highlight the **move down vertically** arrow and set the speed to **2**.

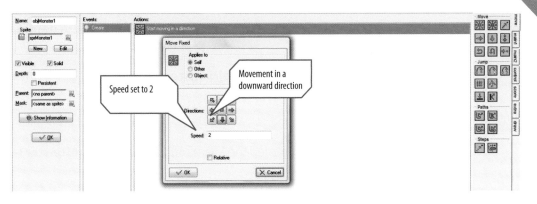

Figure 3.5

3 Now **Add Event** > **Collision** with **objWall** and drag in the **Reverse Vertical** icon as shown in Figure 3.6.

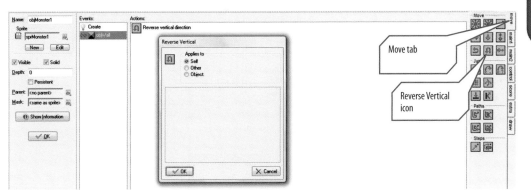

Figure 3.6

Leave the setting as **Self** and click on **OK**.

We must now set the same event for a collision with **objPacman**.

4 Select **Add Event** > **Collision** with **objPacman** and drag in the **Reverse Vertical** icon.

Again, leave the setting as **Self**.

The Events for Monster1 should be like those shown in Figure 3.7.

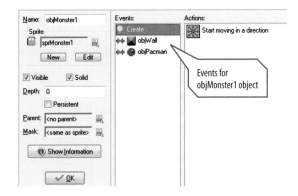

Figure 3.7

Click on **OK** to close the properties window.

⑤ Save the game in the Task3 folder as Task3 and click on the **Run game in debug mode** icon to test it.

Check that the motion is reversed when **objMonster1** collides with **objPacman** and **objWall**.

Yes, it's working.

OK, we have successfully programmed the events and actions for **objMonster1**.

If we look at our plan, **objMonster3** has to move in exactly the same way – downwards, reversing its direction if it collides with **objWall** or **objPacman**.

We could program these again for **objMonster3** in the same way we did for **objMonster1**, but a simpler way is to duplicate (copy) **objMonster1** and then change the sprite. So let's do that.

⑥ Right click on **objMonster3** in the **Objects** folder and select **Delete**.

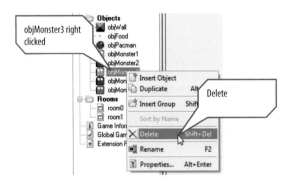

Figure 3.8

You will be shown a dialogue box asking if you want to delete this object.

Click on **Yes**.

⑦ Now right click on **objMonster1** and select **Duplicate**.

A copy of objMonster1 will be created and its properties window will open.

⑧ Change the name to **objMonster3** and change the sprite to **sprMonster3** as shown in Figure 3.9.

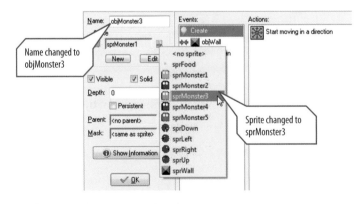

Figure 3.9

FUNCTIONAL SKILLS

Working efficiently – we should think about methods of working that will save time and effort so that we can carry out tasks more efficiently. In this task we can duplicate an object and edit the copy instead of having to repeat programming events and actions for all five monsters

SOFTWARE SKILLS

Deleting an object

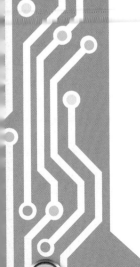

SOFTWARE SKILLS

Duplicating an object

Click on **OK** to close the properties window.

9 We will now have to replace **objMonster3** in the room, as it disappeared when we deleted it in item 6. So select **objMonster3** and click in the top right-hand cell.

10 Save the game and click on the **Run game in debug mode** icon to test it.

Both **objMonster1** and **objMonster3** should behave in the same way.

The other three monsters, 2, 4 and 5, also behave in the same way as each other.

So we can program **objMonster2** and then duplicate and rename it as **objMonster4** and **objMonster5**.

It is more efficient and saves time.

11 Double click **objMonster2** in the **Objects** folder to open its properties window.

12 Select **Add Event** > **Create** and drag in the Move Fixed icon.

Select the move **left** arrow and set the speed to **2**.

Click on **OK**.

13 Select **Add Event** > **Collision** and select **objWall**.

14 Drag in the **Reverse Horizontal** icon and click on **OK**.

15 Select **Add Event** > **Collision** and select **objPacman**.

16 Drag in the **Reverse Horizontal** icon and click on **OK**.

17 Finally click on **OK** to close the properties window.

We can now duplicate this object as **objMonster4** and **objMonster5**.

18 Right click on **objMonster4** and **objMonster5** and delete them.

19 Now right click on **objMonster2** and select **Duplicate**.

> Change the name of the duplicate to **objMonster4**.

> Change the sprite to **sprMonster4**.

Click on **OK** to close the properties window.

20 Repeat item 19 to replace **objMonster5**.

We will now have to reposition **objMonster4** and **objMonster5**. Have a look at Figure 3.4 if you have forgotten where they go.

21 Save the game and click on the **Run game in debug mode** icon to test it.

Yes, all of the monsters are working as expected. Well done.

We now have to program the events and actions for **objPacman**.

FUNCTIONAL SKILLS

Planning work – before we start a task, we should remind ourselves exactly what is required so that we can carry out the tasks efficiently and not have to go back and change the things we have created or add missing items. Plans are also important if we are working in a team so that another member of the team could create the game to our design

STEP 5: PROGRAMMING EVENTS AND ACTIONS FOR OBJPACMAN

For **objPacman**, we need the following events and actions:

Event	Action
Create event	Set Score to 0 Set Lives to 0 Display Score and Lives
Keyboard events	Move in direction of cursor key and change the sprite to sprRight, sprLeft, sprUp or sprDown
Collision with wall	objPacman must stop moving Play sound Wall
Collision with objFood	Play sound Food Increase Score by 1 Test variable Score If Score = 25 then display a message and move to next room
Collision with objMonster1 to 5	Play sound Monster Decrease Lives by 1 Test variable Lives If Lives = 0 then display a message and restart the game

 Double click **objPacman** in the **Objects** folder to open its properties window.

We will first add and program a **Create** event for **objPacman**. When the game starts we must set the Score to zero and the Lives to 3. We must also display them.

 Click on **Add Event** > **Create**.

 Drag in the **Set Score** icon from the **Score** tab. Leave the new score as zero and click on **OK**.

We have done this before – see page 28.

 Now drag in the **Set Lives** icon. Set the new lives to **3** and click on **OK**.

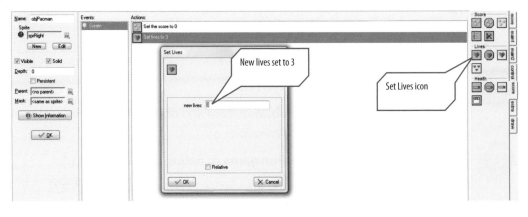

Figure 3.10

5 Drag in the **Score Caption** icon as we have done before.

This time change the **Show lives** option to **show** using the browse icon as in Figure 3.11.

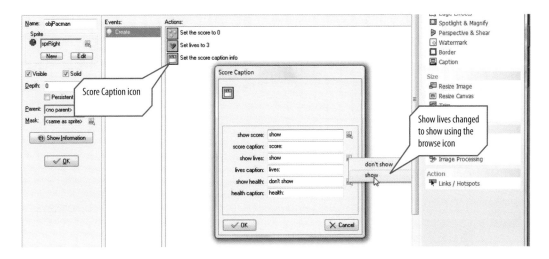

Figure 3.11

Click on **OK**.

We must now create and program key press and key release events for **objPacman**.

We need **objPacman** to move in order to eat the food and to escape from the monsters, but we also want it to stop moving when we stop pressing the cursor keys.

We will start with the right cursor key.

 6 Click on **Add Event** > **Keyboard** > **<Right>**.

For this event we want:

> ❯ **sprRight** to represent the object.

> ❯ **objPacman** to move to the right with a speed of 3.

 7 Drag in the **Move Fixed** icon from the **move** tab.

Select the move **right** arrow and set the speed to **3**.

Click on **OK**.

Now to set the sprite.

 8 Drag in the **Change Sprite** icon from the **main1** tab and select **sprRight** and set the speed to 3 as shown in Figure 3.12.

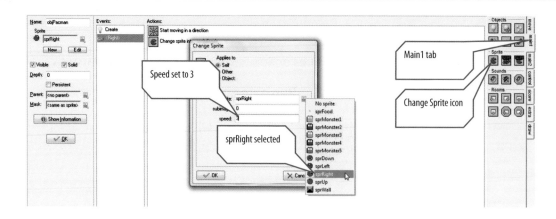

Figure 3.12

Click on **OK**.

 In a similar way, create events and actions for the left, up and down cursor keys.

> For left use sprLeft.

> For up use sprUp.

> For down use sprDown.

Remember to set the motion direction for each object.

Finally, we must stop **objPacman** moving when we release one of the cursor keys.

 Click on **Add Event** > **Key Release** > **<Any key>**.

We must now set the horizontal and the vertical speed to zero.

 Drag in the **Speed Horizontal** icon from the **move** tab, set the speed to zero and click on **OK**.

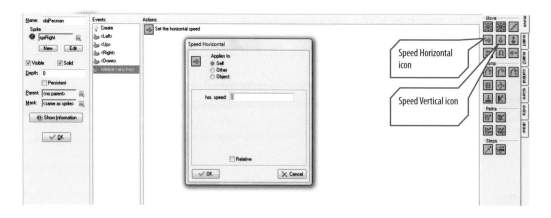

Figure 3.13

12 Repeat item 11 but drag in the **Speed Vertical** icon.

That should be all the events and actions for the movement of **objPacman**.

13 Save the game and click on the **Run game in debug mode** icon to test it.

Check that Pacman moves in the correct directions and that the sprite changes depending on the direction. Also check that it stops moving when the keys are released.

STEP 6: PROGRAMMING COLLISION EVENTS AND ACTIONS FOR OBJPACMAN

Now that we have created events to move the Pacman we must create events for collisions of the Pacman with other objects.

According to our plan, objPacman can collide with:

❯ objWall.

❯ objFood.

❯ objMonster1 to 5.

We will start with collisions with the wall. When this happens, Pacman must stop. So this should be easy.

1 Ensure that the properties window of **objPacman** is still open and select **Add Event** > **Collision** > **objWall**.

We must set the horizontal and vertical speed to zero, just as we set it to 3 when the cursor keys are pressed.

2 Drag in the **Speed Horizontal** icon and set the speed to zero. (See Figure 3.13.)

3 Drag in the **Speed Vertical** icon and set the speed to zero. (See Figure 3.13.)

This will make **objPacman** stop whenever it hits a wall, whether it is travelling in a horizontal or vertical direction.

We now need to add the sound we created earlier.

4 Drag in the **Play Sound** icon from the **main1** tab and select the **Wall** sound file we created earlier.

Then click on **OK**.

We will now create the event of a collision with **objFood**.

When this occurs:

> The instance of objFood should be destroyed.

> The Score should increase by 1.

> The Score should be tested.

> A message should be given to the player saying that they have won and the next room should be loaded if the score is equal to 25.

OK, let's do it.

Select **Add Event** > **Collision** > **objFood**.

Drag in **Destroy Instance** from the **main1** tab.

Select **Other**, as we want **objFood** to be destroyed and not **objPacman**.

Click on **OK**.

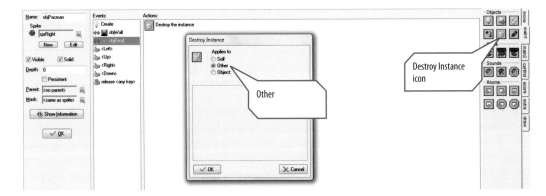

Figure 3.14

We must now increase the Score by one.

Select the **score** tab and drag in the **Set Score** icon.

Enter **1** as the **new score**.

Click the **Relative** box so that 1 will be added to the existing score.

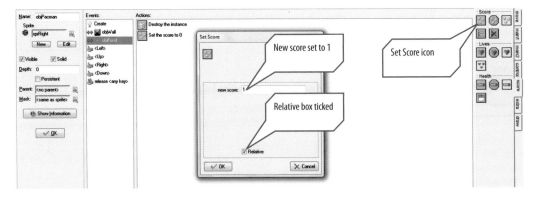

Figure 3.15

Click on **OK**.

We must now test the score to see if it is equal to 25. If it is, we must insert the actions to add a message and then to move to the next room.

Drag in the **Test Score** icon from the **score** tab.

Enter 25 as the **value** and leave **equal to** as the operation.

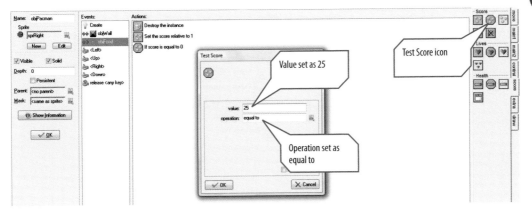

Figure 3.16

Click on **OK**.

Directly under this IF statement we must state what should happen if the score is equal to 25.

If the score is equal to 25, we must add the following actions:

> Display a message saying that the player has won this level.

> Move to the next room.

Because there are two actions, we must put them in a block.

Select the **control** tab, drag in the **Start Block** icon and place it under the **Test Score** icon.

Figure 3.17

Now drag in the **Display Message** icon from the **main2** tab and enter a suitable message.

Click on **OK**.

Now drag in the **Next Room** icon from the **main1** tab and click on **OK**.

12 Finally, drag in the **End Block** icon from the **control** tab.

 13 We must now play the sound for this event, so drag in the **Play Sound** icon and select the **Food** sound. We did this for the **Wall** sound in item 4 above.

The actions for this event should be like those shown in Figure 3.18.

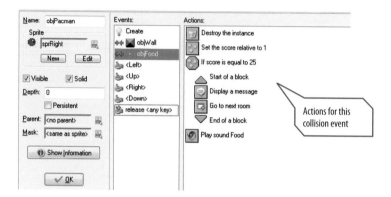

Figure 3.18

 14 Save the game and click on the **Run game in debug mode** icon to check that:

> The food object is destroyed.

> The score increases by 1.

> The sound is played whenever Pacman collides with **objFood**.

We now have to create the collision events with the monsters and program the actions.

 15 Select **Add Event** > **Collision** > **objMonster1**.

 16 Drag in the **Play Sound** icon and select the **Monster** sound.

 17 Drag in the **Set Lives** icon from the **score** tab.

Set the **new lives** to **-1** and click in the **Relative** box.

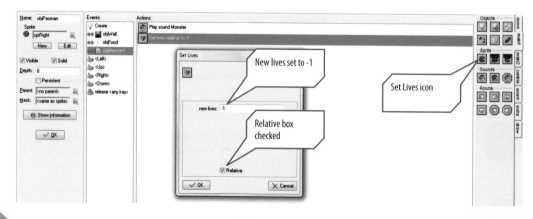

Figure 3.19

Click on **OK**.

We must now check the number of lives remaining.

 18 Drag in the **Test Lives** icon.

Leave the **value** at zero and the **operation** as **equal to**, and click on **OK**.

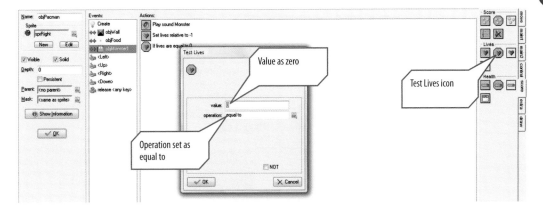

Figure 3.20

Click on **OK**.

We must now program what will happen if the number of lives is equal to zero.

We must:

> Display a message saying that the player has lost.

> Restart the game.

 19 Drag in the **Start Block** icon.

 20 Drag in the **Display Message** icon, enter a message saying that all the lives have been lost and then click on **OK**.

 21 Drag in the **Restart Game** icon.

 22 Drag in the **End Block** icon.

Click on **OK**.

We have programmed the collision event for a collision with **objMonster1** and now we must do this for monsters 2 to 5.

Luckily, we don't have to do this all again as we can duplicate this event and insert the other monsters.

 23 Right click on the **Collision event with object objMonster1** event and select **Duplicate Event**.

 24 Click on **Collision** and select **objMonster2**.

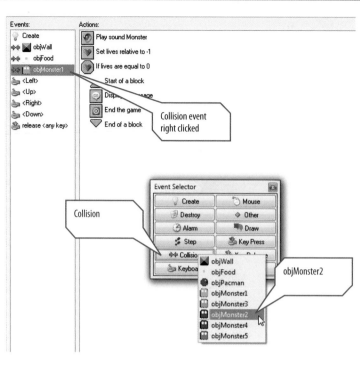

Figure 3.21

This new event with all of the actions will be added to the Events list.

 Repeat items 23 and 24 to create the collision events with monsters 3 to 5.

The events for **objPacman** should now be as shown in Figure 3.22.

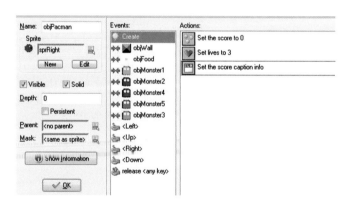

Figure 3.22

All we need to do now is to create a new room for the player to move to if they score 25 points.

STEP 7: CREATING A NEW ROOM

 Open the **Rooms** folder and right click on **room0**.

Select **Duplicate**.

The room has been duplicated.

We now have to duplicate **objPacman** and all of the monster objects.

3 Right click on **objPacman** in the **Objects** folder and select **Duplicate**.

4 Rename the duplicate as **objPacman_2** as shown in Figure 3.23 and then click on **OK** to close the properties window.

Figure 3.23

5 Now duplicate all of the monster objects, renaming them as:

➤ objMonster1_2

➤ objMonster2_2

➤ objMonster3_2

➤ objMonster4_2

➤ objMonster5_2

6 Remove **objPacman** and all of the monster objects from **room1** by right clicking on them and replace them with their duplicates in the same positions.

We will now have to edit the collision events of these new objects in **room1**, because currently they refer to objects in **room0**.

We will start with the collision events for **objPacman_2**.

7 Double click **objPacman_2** in the **Objects** folder to open its properties window.

Right click on the **Collision Event with object objMonster1** and select **Change Event** as shown in **Figure 3.24**.

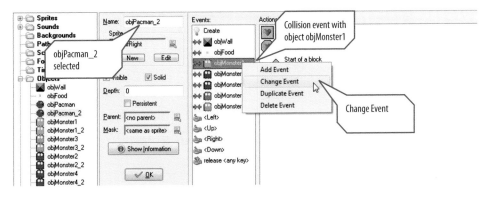

Figure 3.24

Click on the **Collision** event and select **objMonster1_2** (Figure 3.25).

Now change the other monster collision events as shown in Figure 3.26.

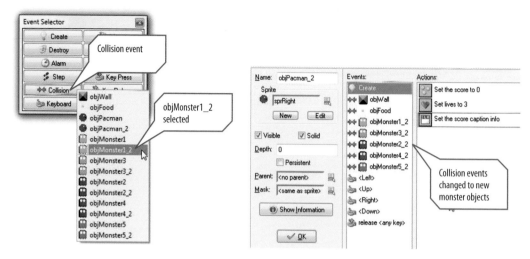

Figure 3.25   *Figure 3.26*

Click on **OK** to close the properties window of **objPacman_2**.

We will now have to change the collision events for the new monster objects to collisions with **objPacman_2** instead of **objPacman**.

Double click on **objMonster1_2** in the **Objects** folder.

Right click on the **Collision Event with object objPacman** panel and select **Change Event**.

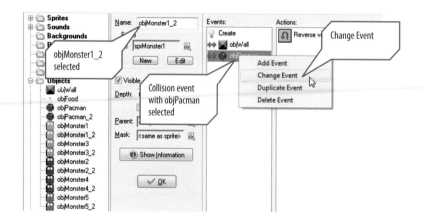

Figure 3.27

Click on the **Collision** event, select **objPacman_2** and then click on **OK** to close the properties window.

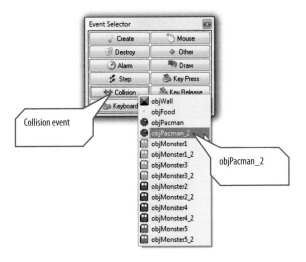

Figure 3.28

 13 Repeat item 11 for all of the new monsters

➤ objMonster2_2

➤ objMonster3_2

➤ objMonster4_2

➤ objMonster5_2

so that they now collide with **objPacman_2**.

 14 All you now have to do is to make some changes to this room.

You could:

➤ Remove some of the **objFood** instances.

➤ Place them in more inaccessible areas.

➤ Make the monsters move more quickly.

➤ Add more monsters.

You will also have to change the message in this room if the player gains a score of 25 in the **Collision Event with object objFood**.

If the player gains a score of 25 you should change the message to tell the player that they have won the game and then use the **End Game** icon instead of the **Next Room** icon as shown in Figure 3.29.

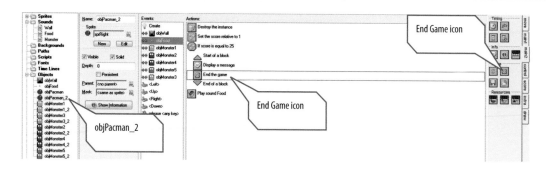

Figure 3.29

STEP 8: TESTING AND EVALUATING THE GAME

 Save the game again and then click on the **Run game in debug mode** icon.

 Test all aspects of the game, especially that the messages are shown when the score equals 25 or when all three lives are lost.

3 We must also check that the game meets all of the client's requirements.

Requirement	Met?
The Pacman character should be able to move in four directions using the cursor keys and always face the way it is moving.	✓
At the start of the game, Pacman should have three lives and lose one if it collides with a monster.	✓
When all three lives have been lost, the player should receive a message telling them that they have lost the game and it should then restart.	✓
If a monster hits a wall, it should reverse its direction.	✓
There should be food items for the Pacman character to eat and they should gain a point for each item.	✓
When the player has gained a certain number of points, they should move to a harder game level.	✓
The game should have sound.	✓

Well done! We have met all of the requirements.

 Either use **File** > **Create Executable** or use the **Create a stand-alone executable for your game** icon on the toolbar to use the game.

CHECKPOINT

Check that you can:

> Change the sprite used for an object during the game

> Set and display the number of lives

> Test the number of lives

> Test the score

> Reverse the direction of movement of an object

> Move to a new room when the points reach a certain number

ASSESSMENT POINT

Now let's assess the work. Look back at the table at the beginning of this section (**Target point**) and decide on which of the statements you can answer 'Yes' to.

Did you do as well as you expected? Could you improve your work? Add a comment to your work to show what you could do to improve it so that next time you'll remember to do it the first time.

Task 4
CREATING A SPACE INVADERS GAME

TASK BRIEF

The company has accepted the Pacman game you submitted. They are impressed with the way you designed the stages and tested and evaluated your work. They would now like you to submit designs for their final new game and have sent you the following email.

From: Big Games Ltd

To: The Game Design Studio

BACKGROUND

Big Games Ltd would like you to submit plans for a Space Invaders game. This should again be aimed at inexperienced players between the ages of six and ten.

TASK REQUIREMENTS

 1 The aliens should start at the top of the screen and gradually move down.

 2 The shooter object should move along the bottom of the screen and fire missiles at the aliens.

 3 If a missile hits an alien, it should explode and disappear.

 4 Every time an alien is destroyed, the player should gain 1 point. The player wins the game if a certain score is reached.

 5 If the aliens reach the bottom of the screen, the player loses the game.

 6 There should be two types of aliens and the second type cannot be destroyed until all of the first type has been destroyed.

 7 The game should have sound.

We invite The Game Design Studio to create a game to meet these requirements.

As you create the game to meet these requirements, you will use the software skills and capability you developed in the last tasks and cover the following new ones:

SOFTWARE SKILLS

You will be able to:

> *Create and use animated sprites*
> *Destroy the objects when the animation has finished*
> *Use a variable to test the number of aliens destroyed*

FUNCTIONAL SKILLS

As you work through this task, the Functional Skills tabs will explain to you why the task tackles the brief in the way shown here and explain why you would choose to:

> *Design and plan your work*
> *Select appropriate media files*
> *Test and evaluate your work*

CAPABILITY

You will show that you can:

> Create a game to meet the requirements
> Select suitable images to be used as sprites
> Select suitable sounds
> Formulate the rules needed for the game
> Program series of events and actions to obey these rules

VOCABULARY

You should learn this new word and understand what it means:

> Animated sprite

RESOURCES

There are two files of a similar game to what you should have produced by the end of this task:

Task4.gmk – a Game Maker file that can be used and edited in the program.

Task4.exe – an executable file of the game.

You can download these files from www.payne-gallway.co.uk

Level 3	Level 4	Level 5	Level 6
You have created a new file and saved it as 'Task4' in the Task4 folder	You have searched, selected and created suitable sprites for the game	You have created events and actions to check the positions of the objects	You have created a variable
You have created a new room	You have created objects using the sprites	You have created events to increase the score	You have used the variable to test the number of aliens destroyed
You have created sprites	You have arranged the objects within the room	You have created an event to convert one object into another	Your game meets all of the requirements
You have created objects	You have created events for the movement of the objects	You have created an event to destroy an animated sprite when it has run	
	You have set and displayed the score	You have created an event to restart the game	

TARGET POINT

Have a look at the following statements before you start your task so you know what you are aiming for.

In this task you will be required to make some decisions for yourself, because items covered in Tasks 1, 2 and 3 will not be repeated in this task.

OK. Let's get started.

Before you start any task, you should organise your area where you are going to save the work.

Create a folder called 'Task4' inside the Game Making folder – this is where you will save the file you will be creating in this task.

STEP 1: DESIGNING THE GAME

To meet the client's requirements we will need:

> Two types of alien.

> A shooter object.

> A missile object.

> An explosion object, because when an alien is hit it must turn into an explosion.

That should be easy for us to do, but we have three more difficult tasks to complete:

> We have to use an animated sprite for the explosion and then make it disappear when the animation has run.

> We need to keep track of where the aliens are on the screen because if they reach the bottom of the screen, the player has lost the game. We will need to use the **Step** event to keep track of this.

> We need to keep track of how many of the first type of alien have been destroyed, as they all have to have been hit before the second type can be destroyed. We will need to create a new variable for this.

We also need to design all of the objects, events and actions. The table below shows how the game will meet these requirements.

Object	Events	Actions
Shooter object	Right cursor key pressed	Shooter moves to right Stops if at right of room
	Left cursor key pressed	Shooter moves to left Stops if at left of room
	Space bar	Missile is created
Missile	Create	Moves up the window
Alien1	Create	Moves down the window
	Collision with missile	Score increases by 1 Variable increases by 1 Missile object destroyed Alien1 object replaced by explosion object
	Step	Test the y coordinate of the object
Alien2	Create	Moves down the window
	Collision with missile	Score increases by 1 Test the score Missile object destroyed Alien2 object replaced by explosion object
	Step	Test the y coordinate of the object
Explosion	Animation end	Destroy the object

FUNCTIONAL SKILLS

Plans and designs are important because:

- *They show all of your ideas so you could easily present them to your client, and they are easy and cheap to change if your client doesn't like them*

- *When the project is under way, you can keep looking back at the documents to make sure you have done everything you needed to*

STEP 2: SELECTING SPRITES

For this game we need sprites for the following objects:

- Alien1.
- Alien2.
- Explosion – animated sprite.
- Missile.
- Shooter.

If you look at the sprites supplied with the game in the **Game_Maker7\Sprites** folder, you will see that there are four sub-folders. You can use any of these sprites for this game.

In the game, the **Burger** image in the **Game_Maker7\Sprites\various** folder is going to be used for the Alien1 object. It is going to be edited for Alien2. The game is going to be called 'Attack of the Killer Burgers'.

The **Bear** image is going to be used as the sprite for the shooter object and the **Dot** image is going to be used for the missile.

Because there isn't a suitable animation to use for the explosion object – we will have to create one.

In addition to the sprites supplied with the game you can find plenty of others by searching the Internet using suitable keyword searches. Try searching the official Game Maker website, which has lots of resources provided by the large Game Maker community around the world.

If you enter the following URL you will find plenty of suitable sprites for your game: **http://www.yoyogames.com/make/resources**.

These resource packs can be downloaded to your computer or area on the network.

The tutorials that you can download from the site contain sprites that you can use in other games.

Tutorials can be found at the following URL: **http://www.yoyogames.com/make/tutorials**.

There are plenty of other sites around the world which provide help with Game Maker.

STEP 3: CREATING SPRITES

1 Use suitable graphics to create the following sprites:

> ❯ sprShooter

> ❯ sprMissile

> ❯ sprAlien1

For the game in this task, use the images listed in Step 2 from the **Game_ Maker7\Sprites\various** folder.

For **Alien2**, the image is going to be an edited version of the one used for **Alien1**.

2 Create a new sprite and load the same image as used for **sprAlien1** – in this case, the burger image.

Name it as **sprAlien2** and click on **Edit Sprite**.

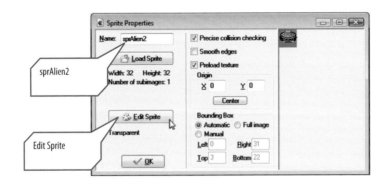

Figure 4.1

The **Sprite Editor** will open.

3 Double click the image to open the **Image Editor**.

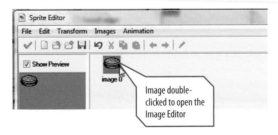

Figure 4.2

This image is going to be edited by using a red fill on the burger, but you could edit it in other ways.

4 Select the **Fill** tool and then the red fill.

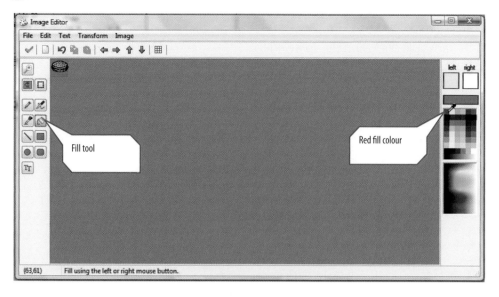

Figure 4.3

 5 Fill the burger with the red colour by left clicking on it.

6 When you are happy with your editing, click on the green **Close, saving the changes** icon.

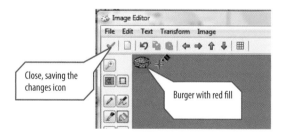

Figure 4.4

You will be returned to the **Sprite Editor**.

7 Click on the **OK, save changes** icon.

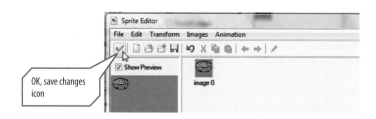

Figure 4.5

8 Finally, click on **OK** to close the sprite properties window of **sprAlien2**.

We now need an animated sprite for the explosion. If you search carefully you should be able to find one on a website, but for this game we are going to create a simple one using the sprite editor.

 9 Click on the **Create a sprite** icon on the toolbar and then, without loading a sprite, click on **Edit Sprite**.

You will see that the image has a background but nothing on it – a blank canvas for our artwork.

 10 This is going to be an explosion, so we will make it a larger image.

Choose **Transform** > **Resize Canvas**.

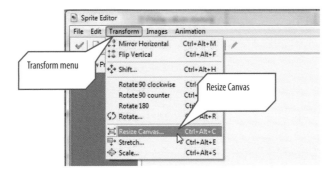

Figure 4.6

11 Change the size to 64 × 64 pixels as shown in Figure 4.7 and click on **OK**.

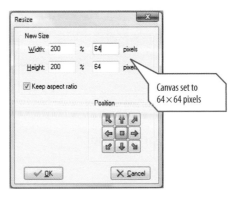

Figure 4.7

 12 Now double click the image to open the **Image Editor**.

 13 Select the **Ellipse** tool and the **yellow** fill colour, as shown in Figure 4.8.

Starting at the top left-hand corner of the canvas, draw a circle as shown in Figure 4.8.

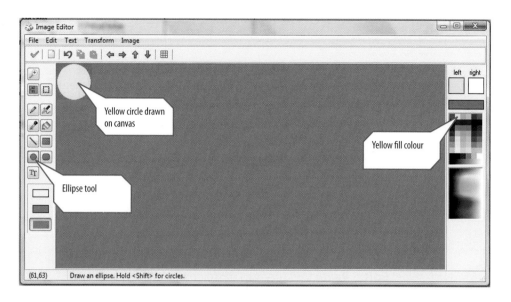

Figure 4.8

14 Click on the **Close, saving the changes** icon to return to the **Sprite Editor**.

Now for the clever bit. The **Sprite Editor** is going to convert this into an animation starting with a tiny circle that grows into the one that we have drawn. We just have to tell it how many steps we want.

15 Select **Animation** > **Grow** > **Center** (Figure 4.9).

You will now be asked how many frames you want for this animation.

16 Enter **6** and click on **OK** (Figure 4.10).

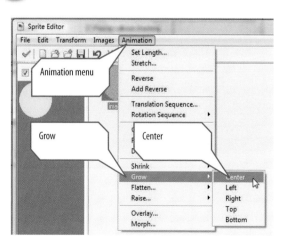

Figure 4.9

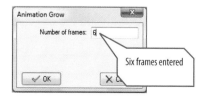

Figure 4.10

You will now see the images for your animation. If the **Show Preview** box is ticked you will see the actual animation.

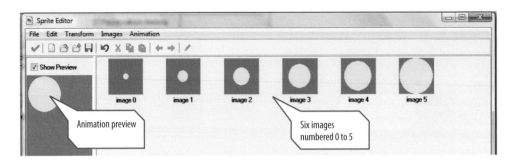

Figure 4.11

 Click on image **5** to select it and then select **Edit** > **Copy**.

 Now select **Edit** > **Paste** four times to paste images 6 to 9.

We are going to edit these images to make the explosion gradually get smaller.

 Double click **image 6** to open the **Image Editor**.

> Select the **Ellipse** tool.

> Select the background fill.

> Draw a small circle in the centre of the larger yellow one.

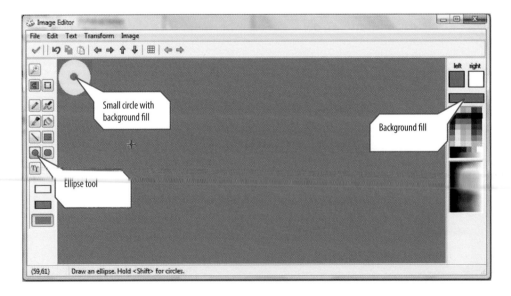

Figure 4.12

Click on the **Close, saving the changes** icon to return to the **Sprite Editor**.

20 Repeat item 19 for images 7–9, gradually making the central circle larger as shown in Figure 4.13.

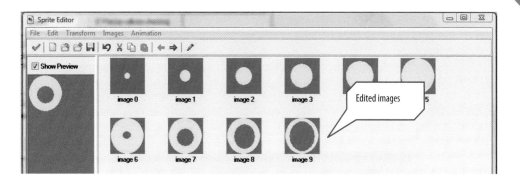

Figure 4.13

 21 Click on the **OK, save changes** icon.

 22 Name the sprite as **sprExplosion** and click on **OK** to close the properties window.

That should be all of the sprites we need.

STEP 4: CREATING OBJECTS

 1 You should be familiar with creating objects by now so for this game you'll need to create the following objects.

Object	Sprite used
objShooter	sprShooter
objMissile	sprMissile
objAlien1	sprAlien1
objAlien2	sprAlien2
objExplosion	sprExplosion

STEP 5: CREATING A SOUND

 1 For this game we need only one sound and that's for the explosion.

Create a sound called **Explosion** and find a suitable sound file from **Game_Maker7\Sounds**.

STEP 6: CREATING A ROOM

 1 Create a new room and change the grid size to 32 × 32 pixels.

 2 Arrange **objShooter** in the centre of the bottom row and add instances of **objAlien1** and **objAlien2** at the top of the room.

FUNCTIONAL SKILLS

Combining files – we should chose sounds that are appropriate to the action that is occurring in the game. A beep would not be appropriate for a collision between a missile and an alien. We need an explosion sound

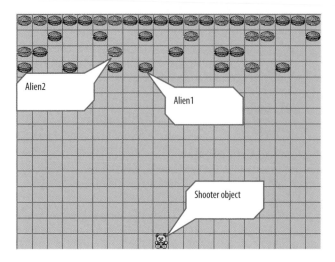

Figure 4.14

STEP 7: CREATING A SPLASH SCREEN

Although it wasn't in the client's requirements, we can improve the overall presentation of the game by creating a splash screen as we did for Task 1. It should also impress our clients and improve our chances of winning the contract!

 Create a new room and rename it as **Splash**.

 Rename the original room as **Game** and drag the **Splash** room so that it is above the Game room.

Remember that the dimensions are 624 × 464 pixels and create an image in a graphics program with those dimensions.

 Create a new background, load the image you have just created and click on **OK**.

 Make sure that the **Splash** room is selected, click on the **backgrounds** tab and select the background you have just created.

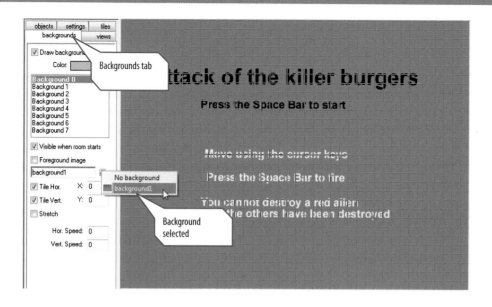

Figure 4.15

 Create an object without a sprite and name it **objControl**.

Click on **Add Event** > **Keyboard** > **<Space>**, drag in the **Next Room** icon and add a transition.

 Add this event to the **Splash** room.

 Save the game as 'Task4' and click on the **Run game in debug mode** icon to check that it is working as expected.

Now we can start to create the events and program the actions for the **Game** room.

STEP 8: CREATING THE EVENTS AND ACTIONS FOR OBJSHOOTER

Before we start, we should remind ourselves what is needed for this object.

Events	Actions
Create	Set score to 0 Display score Create a variable to count number of Alien1 objects destroyed Set this variable to 0
Left cursor key	Move to the left Stop if at extreme left of room
Right cursor key	Move to the right Stop if at extreme right of room
Space Bar	Create an instance of the missile object

FUNCTIONAL SKILLS

Planning work – before we start a task, we should remind ourselves exactly what is required so that we can carry out the tasks efficiently and don't have to go back and change the things we have created or add missing items

At the start of the game, when **objShooter** is created, we must set the score to 0 and also create a variable to count the number of **Alien1** objects that have been destroyed.

1 Double click on **objShooter** in the **Objects** folder to open its properties window.

2 Click on **Add Event** > **Create**.

3 Drag in the **Set Score** icon, leave the new score as zero and click on **OK**.

4 Drag in the **Score Caption** icon and click on **OK**.

We must now create a new variable to count how many **Alien1** objects have been destroyed.

We will name the variable as **Alien1**.

5 Drag in the **Execute Code** icon from the **control** tab.

Enter

globalvar Alien1;

as the code to execute. This creates a global variable called **Alien1**.

We make the variable global so that it can be seen and used by other objects.

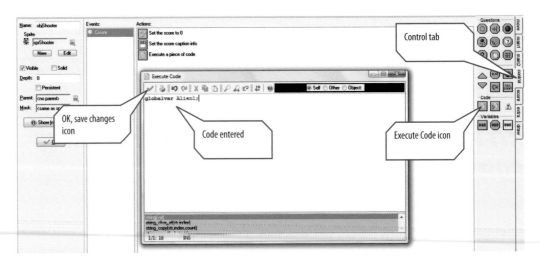

Figure 4.16

Click on the **OK, Save changes** icon.

We must now set this variable to zero.

6 Drag in the **Set Variable** icon.

Enter **Alien1** as the variable and set the value to zero, as shown in Figure 4.17.

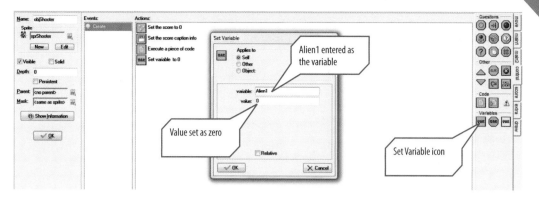

Figure 4.17

Click on **OK**.

We must now add the keyboard events for **objShooter**. We want it to move left and right only if it is not at the extreme left and right of the room. This time we will program these in a different way by making the object jump four pixels at a time. We can check if it at the left or right by checking the X coordinate.

 Click on **Add Event** and select **Keyboard** > **<Left>**.

We want **objShooter** to jump to the left only if the X coordinate is greater than 0.

 Drag in the **Test Expression** icon and enter **x>0** (x is greater than zero) as the expression to test.

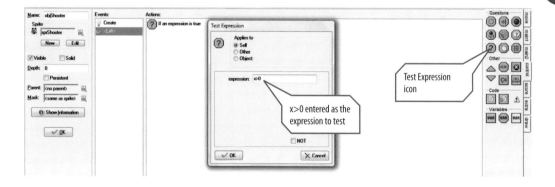

Figure 4.18

Click on **OK**.

Immediately under this icon we must state what should happen if x is greater than 0.

 Drag in the **Jump to Position** icon from the **move** tab, as shown in Figure 4.19.

Enter **-4** in the **x** field – it is a minus value because we want it to move to the left.

Click in the **Relative** box, or **objShooter** will jump to the top of the window.

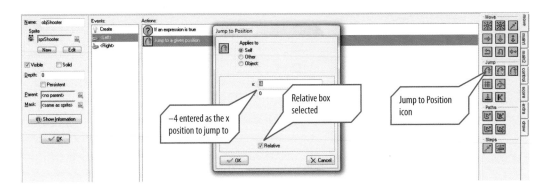

Figure 4.19

Click on **OK**.

We must now create a similar event and actions for moving to the right, but this time we will have to check that x is less than 608.

 Click on **Add Event** and select **Keyboard** > **<Right>**.

 Drag in the **Test Expression** icon and enter **x<608** (x is less than 608) as the expression to test.

 Drag in the **Jump to Position** icon from the **move** tab.

> Enter **4** in the **x** field – we want it to move to the right.

> Tick the **Relative** box, or **objShooter** will jump to the top of the window as y is zero.

> Click on **OK**.

 Save the game and click on the **Run game in debug mode** icon to check that it is working as expected.

The last event for **objShooter** is when the space bar is pressed. A new missile has to be created.

When the space bar is pressed a new instance of **objMissile** has to be created at the **objShooter** position.

 Click on **Add Event** and select **Keyboard** > **<Space>**.

 Drag in the **Create Instance** icon from the **main1** tab, as shown in Figure 4.20.

> Select **objMissile** as the object.

> Leave the **x** and **y** coordinates as 0.

> Tick the **Relative** box or the instance will be created in the top left-hand corner.

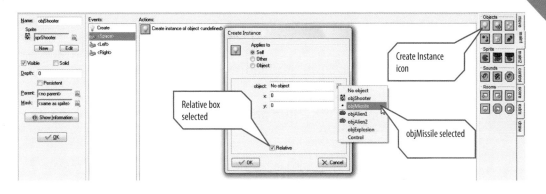

Figure 4.20

We must now create an event for the new instance of **objMissile** when it is created.

We want it to move upwards.

 Click on **OK** to close the properties window of **objShooter**.

 Double click **objMissile** in the Objects folder to open its properties window.

 Click on **Add Event** and select **Create**.

 Drag in the **Speed Vertical** icon from the **move** tab.

> Set the **vert speed** to **-3**. It is a negative number as we want the missile to move upwards.

> Click on **OK**.

> Click on **OK** to close the properties window.

 Save the game and click on the **Run game in debug mode** icon to check that it is working as expected.

Check that a new missile is created when the space bar is pressed and that it moves upwards.

objShooter moves to the left and right and missiles are launched when the space bar is pressed.

There is, however, one problem. If the player keeps the space bar pressed down and moves **objShooter** to the left or right, a line of missiles is created. This makes the game too easy.

We can overcome this by changing the event.

 Double click on **objShooter** and right click on the **<Space>** event.

Select **Delete Event**.

Click **Yes** to confirm.

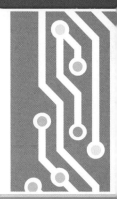

Click on **Add Event** and select **Key Press** > **<Space>**.

 Repeat item 15 above to create an instance of **objMissile**.

 Save the game and click on the **Run game in debug mode** to check that it is working as expected.

That's better. The player now can't keep the space bar pressed down to create a stream of missiles!

Now we just need events and actions for the alien objects.

FUNCTIONAL SKILLS

Planning work – before we start a task, we should remind ourselves exactly what is required so that we can carry out the tasks efficiently and not have to go back and change the things we have created or add missing items. Plans are also important if we are working in a team, so that another member of the team could create the game to our design

STEP 9: CREATING THE MOVEMENT EVENTS FOR THE ALIEN OBJECTS

Let's remind ourselves how the aliens have to move.

When the game starts, they have to move down the room.

The **Step** event will track if they have reached the bottom – the Y coordinate will be greater than 448 when they are.

If the Y coordinate is greater than 448, a message should be displayed saying that the player has lost the game and the game should restart.

Not too difficult! So let's see how it's done.

 Double click **objAlien1** to open its properties window.

 Click on **Add Event** and select **Create**.

When the object is created we have to set the vertical speed.

 Drag in the **Speed Vertical** icon from the **move** tab and set the **vert speed** to 0.2

Click on **OK**.

 Click on **Add Event** and select **Step** > **Step**.

This event will check the object 'every step of the game'.

At every step of the game we want the y coordinate to be checked.

 Drag in the **Test Expression** icon from the **control** tab, as shown in Figure 4.21.

Enter **y>448** as the expression to test.

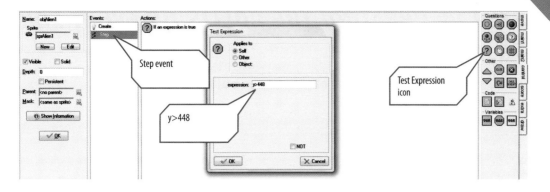

Figure 4.21

Click on **OK**.

We must now program what should happen **if** y **is** greater than 448.

 Carry out the following:

> Drag in the **Start Block** icon.

> Drag in the **Display Message** icon and enter a suitable message telling the player that they have lost.

> Drag in the **Restart Game** icon.

> Drag in the **End Block** icon.

> Click on **OK** to close the properties window of **objAlien1**.

Figure 4.22

 Double click on **objAlien2** and repeat items 2–6 above, as the movement of objAlien2 is identical to objAlien1.

 Save the game and click on the **Run game in debug mode** icon to check that it is working as expected.

Check that both types of aliens move down the room together and that the message is displayed when they reach the bottom.

STEP 10: CREATING THE COLLISION EVENT FOR OBJALIEN1

We must create a collision event for **objAlien1** and **objMissile**.

When this occurs we must:

➤ Increase the score by 1.

➤ Destroy the **Missile** instance.

➤ Play the **Explosion** sound.

➤ Increase the **Alien1** variable by 1.

➤ Change the **Alien1** instance into an **Explosion** instance.

 Double click **objAlien1** in the **Objects** folder.

 Click on **Add Event** and select **Collision** > **objMissile**.

 Drag in the **Set Score** icon and set the **new score** to 1.

Click in the **Relative** box.

Click on **OK**.

We do not have to test the score for **Alien1** to see if the player has won the game, since we know that they also have to destroy all of the **Alien2** instances.

 Drag in the **Destroy Instance** icon and select **Other** as the instance to destroy so that the missile is destroyed.

 Drag in the **Play Sound** icon and select the **Explosion** sound.

We must now increase the **Alien1** variable by 1.

 Drag in the **Set Variable** icon.

Enter **Alien1** as the variable and **1** as the value.

Tick the **Relative** box and click **OK**.

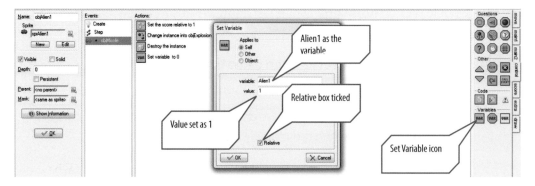

Figure 4.23

7 Drag in the **Change Instance** icon from the **main1** tab.

Select **objExplosion** as the object to **change into**.

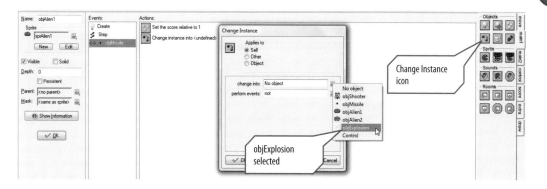

Figure 4.24

Click on **OK**.

That should be all of the events and actions for **objAlien1**.

8 Click on **OK** to close the properties window, save the game and click on the **Run game in debug mode** icon to check that it is working as expected.

Yes, the **Alien1** instances are destroyed and there is an explosion and a sound.

But – yes, there's usually a but – the explosion keeps going on and on.

It should be destroyed after it has run.

We can easily correct this.

STEP 11: DESTROYING OBJEXPLOSION AFTER IT HAS RUN

1 Double click **objExplosion** in the **Objects** folder to open its properties window.

2 Click on **Add Event** and select **Other > Animation end**.

3 Drag in the **Destroy Instance** icon from the **main1** tab, leave it set as **Self** and click on **OK**.

4 Click on **OK** to close the properties window, save the game and click on the **Run game in debug mode** to check that it works again.

Check that the explosion is destroyed and that the score increases by 1 each time.

All we now have to do now is to program the collision event for **objAlien2**.

FUNCTIONAL SKILLS

Editing and refining work – we must always be prepared to edit and refine our work to make it more appropriate for the audience and the requirements. In this case we must change what we have done to make the explosion disappear after the animation has run

SOFTWARE SKILLS
Using the Animation End action

STEP 12: CREATING THE COLLISION EVENT FOR OBJALIEN2

When there is a collision between **objAlien2** and **objMissile** we have to program the following to happen:

Test the variable **Alien1** to check that all of the **Alien1** objects have been destroyed because all of **objAlien1** have to be destroyed before **objAlien2** can be destroyed and counted in the score. In this case, the variable **Alien1** should be equal to 25 because there are 25 instances of **objAlien1**.

If it is equal to 25 we then have to:

❯ Increase the score by 1.

❯ Test the score to see if it is equal to 40, because in this game there are 40 aliens in total that have to be destroyed in order to win the game

  ❯ If it is equal to 40, then display a message telling that the player that they have won.

  ❯ End the game.

❯ Destroy the **Missile** instance.

❯ Play the **Explosion** sound.

❯ Change the **Alien2** instance into an **Explosion** instance.

Let's make a start.

 Double click **objAlien2** in the **Objects** folder to open its properties window.

 Add a **Collision** event with **objMissile**.

 Drag in the **Test Variable** icon from the **control** tab.

Enter **Alien1** as the **variable**.

Enter **25** as the **value**.

Leave the **operation** as **equal to**.

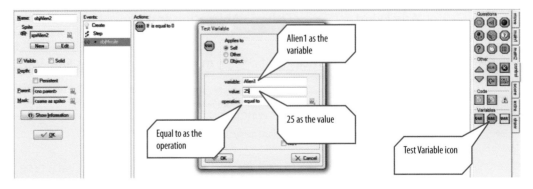

Figure 4.25

102

Click on **OK**.

Drag in the **Start Block** icon from the **control** tab.

We must now create a block of actions to be carried out if **Alien1** is equal to 25.

We have to:

> Increase the score by 1.

> Destroy the **Missile** instance.

> Play the **Explosion** sound.

> Change the **Alien2** instance into an **Explosion** instance.

Drag in the icons to create these actions.

If you are unsure, repeat items 3, 4, 5 and 7 in Step 9 above.

Finally drag in the **End Block** icon.

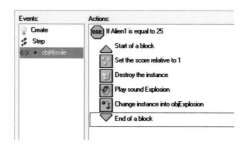

Figure 4.26

We must now test the score to see if it is equal to 40. There are 40 aliens in this game: 25 instances of **objAlien1** and 15 of **objAlien2**.

Drag in the **Test Score** icon from the **Score** tab.

Set the **value** to **40** and leave the **operation** as **equal to**.

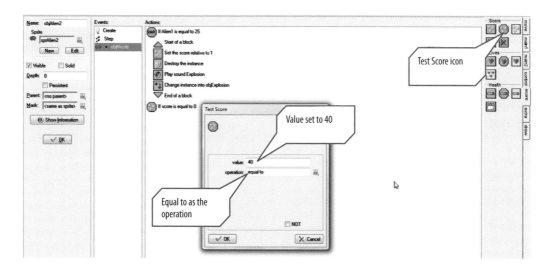

Figure 4.27

We must now program events to occur if the value is equal to 40.

8   Drag in the following icons:

> Start Block.

> Display Message and enter a suitable message telling the player that they have won the game.

> End Game.

> End Block.

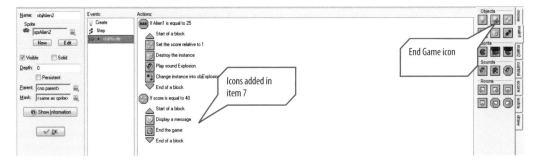

Figure 4.28

Click on **OK** to close the properties window for **objAlien2**.

That should be the game completed.

9   Save the game and click on the **Run game in debug mode** to check it again.

Check that **Alien2** objects can be destroyed after all of the **Alien1** ones have been.

Yes, it works. Well done!

STEP 13: TESTING AND EVALUATING THE GAME

1   We must check that the game meets all of the client's requirements.

Requirement	Met?
The aliens should start at the top of the screen and gradually move down.	✓
The shooter object should move along the bottom of the screen and fire missiles at the aliens.	✓
If a missile hits an alien, it should explode and disappear.	✓
Every time an alien is destroyed the player should gain a point and the player wins the game if a certain score is reached.	✓
If the aliens reach the bottom of the screen, the player loses the game.	✓
There should be two types of aliens and the second type cannot be destroyed until all of the first type have been destroyed.	✓
The game should have sound.	✓

Well done! We have met all of the requirements.

Plus, we have improved on it, because we have added a splash screen!

 2 Either use **File** > **Create Executable** or use the **Create a stand-alone executable for your game** icon on the toolbar to use the game.

CHECKPOINT

Check that you can:

❯ Create and use animated sprites

❯ Destroy the objects when the animation has finished

❯ Use a variable to test the number of aliens destroyed

ASSESSMENT POINT

Now let's assess the work. Look back at the table at the beginning of this section (**Target point**) and decide on which of the statements you can answer 'Yes' to.

Did you do as well as you expected? Could you improve your work? Add a comment to your work to show what you could do to improve it so that next time you'll remember to do it the first time.

CREATING A GAME WITH THREE LEVELS TO MATCH A PROJECT BRIEF

TASK BRIEF

The company have been impressed with the three games that you have submitted, and the way you designed all of the stages and tested and evaluated what you had done. They would now like you to submit designs for a new game and have sent you the following email.

From: Big Games Ltd

To: The Game Design Studio

BACKGROUND

Big Games Ltd would like you to submit plans for a new game aimed at six- to ten-year-olds.

The game can be on any topic but should meet the following requirements:

PROJECT REQUIREMENTS

1 The game should have a title page that introduces the game and gives any instructions that are needed. There should also be sound on this page.

2 When a key is pressed, the game should start.

3 There should be at least three games rooms and no more than five.

4 Each room should have a background that could be a digital photograph or an image you have created.

5 The background image should exactly fit the page.

6 The player should start with five lives and they should be able to score points in each room.

7 When the player gains enough points they should move to the next room.

8 When a player has lost all of their lives, a message should appear telling them they have lost and the game should restart.

9 A message should appear when they have completed all of the rooms and the game should end.

We invite The Game Design Studio to create a game to meet these requirements.

 **TARGET POINT**

Have a look at the following statements before you start your task so you know what you are aiming for.

Level 3	Level 4	Level 5	Level 6
You have created a new file and saved it as 'Project'	You have created three rooms	You have created a game with five rooms	You have created five rooms with backgrounds that exactly fit the room and are appropriate to the theme of the game
You have created one room	You have selected sprites to match the objects used in the game	You have created events and actions to check the positions of the objects	You have selected sprite images that are appropriate for the objects they represent
You have created sprites	You have created objects using the sprites	You have created events to increase the score	You have edited sprite objects to make them appropriate
You have created objects for the game	You have created backgrounds for the rooms	You have created an action to move to a new room when the score reaches a certain number	You have created an animated sprite
	You have programmed an event so that when a key is pressed the game starts	You have created events to check and display the number of lives	You have created a variable
	You have set and displayed the score	You have created events to reduce the number of lives	You have used actions to test the variable
	You have programmed keyboard events to move an object	You have created an event to display a message and restart the game when all the lives have been lost	You have tested all aspects of the game and edited and refined it
	You have programmed an event to display a message	You have created an event to convert one object into another	Your game meets all of the requirements
		You have used animated sprites	
		You have created an event to destroy an animated sprite when it has run	
		You have created an event to restart the game	

The Functional Skills listed below show you the skills you will be demonstrating in your work, but remember you have to know *why* you have chosen to demonstrate them in a particular way and how your choice match you audience and purpose for the documents.

 Planning your documents.

Using suitable software for your game.

➤ Saving your documents with suitable filenames.

➤ Selecting particular images for the backgrounds and the sprites.

➤ Creating rooms and objects to match the game design.

➤ Creating events and actions.

➤ Using and testing variables.

➤ Duplicating actions to increase efficiency.

➤ Testing and reviewing your documents.

Creating a game for a particular purpose and for a particular audience is a big job, but the following steps will help you to work through if.

➤ Step 1: Identify the audience and purpose.

➤ Step 2: Think about ideas that could be suitable for your audience and purpose.

➤ Step 3: Design and plan your game.

➤ Step 4: Create your game.

➤ Step 5: Test your game.

➤ Step 6: Evaluate your game – did it work as well as it could have?

To meet this project brief you need to complete Step 4, but that is only one part of the process that you would need to go through if you were designing this game for a real game developer. The information below shows you how you could go about tackling the other steps in the process. Use the target points to decide how and which of the other steps you want to tackle. The Functional Skills listed above show you the skills that you will be demonstrating in your work, but remember you have to be able to say *why* you have chosen to use them in a particular way.

PLANNING

This game is going to need a lot of planning. You will have to:

➤ Decide on the theme or themes of the game.

➤ You could have one theme with the levels becoming more difficult or you could have a different theme for each room.

➤ Plan the gameplay.

➤ What will happen in each room?

➤ How will points be scored?

➤ How will lives be lost?

➤ How many points will be needed to move to the next level?

When planning this section you could use a storyboard. An example storyboard for planning the gameplay for Task 4 is shown in Figure Project.1.

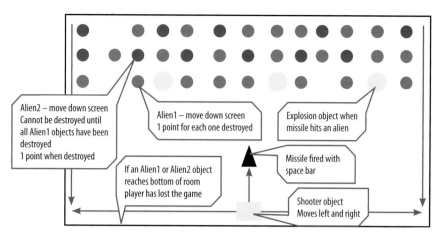

Figure Project.1

❯ List the objects that will be needed for the game.

   ❯ Will walls and barriers be needed?

   ❯ Will there be balls and missiles?

   ❯ Will there be monsters, military equipment, robots, human characters?

You could use a table to help you list these objects like the one below.

Room	Objects
Room 1	objShooter objMissile objAlien1 objAlien2 objExplosion
Room 2	
Room 3	

❯ Make a list of the types of media files you will need.

   ❯ What images will be needed for the backgrounds?

   ❯ Will they be digital photographs or images that you will create?

   ❯ What images will you need for the sprites?

   ❯ Will you search for them on the Internet or create them using the Sprite Editor?

   ❯ What sound files will you need?

You could use a table to help you list these objects like the one below.

File	Use	Source
Image showing sky with clouds	Background for Room 1	Digital photograph
Image of a tank	sprShooter	Game Maker website
Image of a rocket	sprMissile	Created in Sprite Editor
Image of a flying saucer with white fill	sprAlien1	Created in Fireworks
Image of a flying saucer with red fill	sprAlien2	Created in Fireworks
Animation of an explosion	sprExplosion	Created in Sprite Editor
Sound of an explosion	When a missile collides with an alien	From Game Maker website

> Plan all of the events and actions.

> > What events and actions will be needed for the objects?

> > How will the objects move?

> > What will happen when objects collide?

> > How will points be scored?

> > How will the score be tested?

> > How will messages be displayed?

You could use a table to help you list these objects like the one below.

Object	Events	Actions
Shooter object	Right cursor key pressed	Shooter moves to right Stops if right of room
	Left cursor key pressed	Shooter moves to left Stops if at left of room
	Space bar	Missile is created
Missile	Create	Moves up the window
Alien1	Create	Moves down the window
	Collision with missile	Score increases by 1 Variable increases by 1 Missile object destroyed Alien1 object replaced by explosion object
	Step	Test the y coordinate of the object
Alien2	Create	Moves down the window
	Collision with missile	Score increases by 1 Test the score Missile object destroyed Alien2 object replaced by explosion object
	Step	Test the y coordinate of the object
Explosion	Animation end	Destroy the object

The table should list the events and actions in as much detail as possible.

GATHERING THE MEDIA FILES

You will then have to search for, select and edit or create the sound and image files that you will need.

You should create a logical folder structure in your area so that you can locate them easily when you begin to create the game.

CREATING THE GAME

When your plans are complete and you have gathered all of the resources needed, you can start to create the game.

Remember to save the work frequently and make a backup at the end of each session.

Never rely on just one copy of the game – it may become corrupted or there may be a network failure.

TESTING AND EVALUATING

Just as we did during Tasks 1–4, test the game as you are creating it – but remember to save it before each test. You can then correct the events and actions as you go along rather than having to do them all at the end when you may have forgotten exactly what you were trying to do.

Ask as many people as possible for feedback and make changes to the game based on their comments.

You should then evaluate the game against the original requirements. You could use a table similar to the one below to do this:

Requirement	Met?
The game should have a title page that introduces the game and gives any instructions that are needed. There should also be sound on this page.	
When a key is pressed, the game should start.	
There should be at least three games rooms and no more than five.	
Each room should have a background that could be a digital photograph or an image you have created.	
The background image should fit the page exactly.	
The player should start with five lives and they should be able to score points in each room.	
When the player gains enough points, they should move to the next room.	
When a player has lost all of their lives, a message should appear telling them they have lost and the game should restart.	
A message should appear when they have completed all of the rooms and the game should end.	

Finally, you should think of valid ways in which the game could be improved. Do not just state things like 'It should be more exciting' – put down ideas to actually make it more exciting.

From now on, it's up to you. Good luck!

INDEX